THE SUNDERLAND REFRESHING

D0569201

The Sunderland Refreshing

Ken and Lois Gott

Hodder & Stoughton

LONDON SYDNEY AUCKLAND

in association with
New Life Publishing

Copyright © 1995 by Ken and Lois Gott

First published in Great Britain 1995

The right of Ken and Lois Gott to be identified as the Authors
of the Work has been asserted by them in accordance with the
Copyright, Designs and Patents Act 1988.

10 9 8 7 6 5 4

All rights reserved. No part of this publication may be
reproduced, stored in a retrieval system, or transmitted,
in any form or by any means without the prior written
permission of the publisher, nor be otherwise circulated
in any form of binding or cover other than that in which
it is published and without a similar condition being
imposed on the subsequent purchaser.

British Library Cataloguing in Publication Data
A record for this book is available from the British Library

ISBN 0 340 66515 7

Printed and bound in Great Britain by
Cox & Wyman Ltd, Reading, Berkshire

Hodder and Stoughton
A division of Hodder Headline PLC
338 Euston Road
London NW1 3BH
in association with New Life Publishing
PO Box 64
Rotherham
South Yorkshire S60 2YT

Dedication

This book is dedicated to our two favourite people, Debbie and Joanne, our very special daughters, along with our wonderful family at Sunderland Christian Centre.

Acknowledgements

We would like to thank Charles Gardner and
Peter Wreford for their excellent research and
editing of this book, and all the SCC team for
their dedicated help.
Special thanks to Wes Richards for his honesty and
friendship, and Ken Connop for his hard work.

Contents

Foreword

The two people sitting across from me on the sofa looked discouraged and weary. The deep lines cutting around their mouths and the tired look in their eyes were a dead give-away of the sleepless nights and endless battles they had been going through.

A tremendous sense of their 'destiny' took hold of me as I studied their faces and quietly sat praying for God's wisdom to speak into the situation presented to me.

Ken and Lois Gott had a mandate from God, but it was clear to me that the enemy was surely trying to prevent them fulfilling it by taking advantage of all the heartache and pain they had gone through the last few months.

Heartache and pain is something all of us face to a greater or lesser degree in our lives, but I knew from experience that we can make it count for us and use it to our advantage in God! "Help me, Jesus," I softly prayed. "Help me minister that truth to this couple!" Then suddenly a word of wisdom flashed in my spirit... I drew my breath and started to speak...

That morning in 1988 saw the beginning of my friendship with Ken and Lois Gott, a friendship that grew into a relationship of equally sharing, caring and ministering into each other's lives.

Truly God is no respecter of persons! He is in the habit

of taking ordinary people, redirecting their lives and using them as powerful tools for his glory in his kingdom. How wonderful that he takes not only the mighty and powerful, but the humble and obedient, and re-fashions them as trophies of grace and flames of fire.

That I have seen in Ken and Lois. As you read through the chapters of this book, I am sure their experiences will grip you with new intensity and minister hope and faith into your own situation. Joy will burst into your spirit as you see through their story that preparation time is never wasted in God. You will laugh and cry with them as you identify with the wonderful workings of God in their lives. I am sure it will leave you with a hunger to seek the Lord all the more, until nothing else will satisfy you but revival and the salvation of the lost.

Through their openness in sharing their battles and victories, Ken and Lois make you feel a part of the master work of the Holy Spirit in their lives. Like the canvas in the frame of a painter, with Christ himself holding the paintbrush, the Holy Spirit did his marvellous work as they yielded and are yielding to his guidance. Reading this book left me with a fresh appreciation for the intricate, yet master work of the Lord in preparing his people for revival.

As a result of our close friendship over the years, I have had the privilege of having a very direct part in not only the lives of Ken and Lois, but also that of the church they pastor, Sunderland Christian Centre. The people there have opened their lives to me and I in turn have made the church a part of mine. I was introduced to it in its early stages and have witnessed it grow from strength to strength and glory to glory. With great anticipation in my heart, I am praying and believing with them for the day when they are not only used as channels of God's blessings and refreshing to the saints, but as powerful tools in the Master's hand to affect their entire community and nation. For as Jesus said: "The spirit of the Lord is upon me to heal the broken-hearted and to set the captives free." (Isaiah 60:1)

Suzette Hattingh

Associate Evangelist and
Prayer and Intercession Coordinator

Christ for all Nations

Chapter 1

Weird and wonderful

It was almost midnight when the phone rang. Mary Harrison, my mother-in-law, apprehensively picked up the receiver, wondering what kind of urgent need had prompted a call at that late hour.

"Have you got any mints grandma?"

Mary recognised the voice of my 16-year-old daughter Debbie and knew immediately something other than the urgent need for sweets was prompting the request. There had to be more to it. And there was!

Since our houses are adjoining, a rendezvous was arranged at the bottom of the garden.

"Mum and dad are acting very strangely," Debbie said. "Do you think you could come and see if they're all right?"

My daughter's bewilderment at the situation signalled the start of many reports to come of strange and wonderful happenings in Sunderland, England, beginning in the summer of 1994. My wife, Lois, and I had just returned home from Toronto, where we had been powerfully and dramatically touched by the Spirit of God.

What the press have dubbed the 'Toronto Blessing' had come to Sunderland. We now know, however, that the popular coining of the phrase does not reflect that this is in fact God's blessing. The phenomenon which is affecting thousands of churches all over Britain is marked by various unusual manifestations, but most importantly of all a renewed love for Jesus and a love for his people. It took its name from the Toronto Airport Vineyard Church, where the phenomena had broken out in a big way and where Christians from all over the world have made pilgrimages since they began nightly meetings on 20 January 1994.

A visitation not an imitation

Many of those affected appear to have all the symptoms of being drunk without ever having touched alcohol, indeed my own wife Lois had been 'drunk' for four days after receiving prayer in Toronto. On the plane coming home from that extraordinary encounter with God I felt in my heart and spirit that it was most important that neither of us described the manifestations we had seen. If anything was going to happen in our church it had to be of God, not as a result of worked-up emotion. I wanted a visitation not an imitation.

But that didn't alter the fact that when grandma arrived at our home just after midnight on that balmy August evening she witnessed things she had never seen in all her life. Lois, still overcome by the Spirit, kept repeating, 'Now I really know what Acts 2 is all about'. (Jesus's first disciples were accused of being drunk after the Holy Spirit came on them on the day of Pentecost nearly two thousand years ago). I was bent double groaning and making very little sense. Mary reassured the girls, though as she made her way home across the garden she debated how she could explain all she had seen to Herbert, my father-in-law.

For 37 years Herbert Harrison was the senior leader of Bethshan Christian Community Centre in Newcastle, which he pioneered into one of the largest churches in Britain. Now retired, he helps us at our church, Sunderland Christian Centre. His ministry style has always been primarily evangelistic, erring on the side of balance, order and dignity as opposed to great emotional displays. So that evening my in-laws talked long into the night, wondering just what form the Sunday morning service would take, certain that it would be interesting. Recalling a story from the popular press of an organ player who had fallen from his stool, Herbert concluded that should our shy, self-conscious keyboard player Shaun fall from his stool it would most certainly be an act of God. With that they fell asleep.

A Mount Sinai experience

Next morning James Senior, our youth pastor, who had visited Toronto with us, shared with the people that if God was living somewhere in the world at that moment, he felt he had just been to his house. It had been a Mount Sinai experience. Then he broke down and wept and wept before the people. That Sunday morning service was crucial for Lois and me. Amidst all the laughing, shaking, jerking and carpet time in Toronto, God had shown us that in our ignorance we had not given him his church. We ourselves had held it very tightly and selfishly with all ministry flowing from us and all roads leading to us. We needed to step back, repent, let God be the focus and allow ministry to be released to the whole body of Christ.

As Lois began to say sorry to the people laughter broke

out everywhere. There was a massive outpouring of the Spirit that morning and, yes, the first manifestation of all, Shaun fell from his stool into the small orchestra pit built for our musicians. We have since closed it up – it became altogether too dangerous. Before my very eyes our congregation were shaking, jerking, shouting for the Lord to forgive them – in fact, everything just as we'd seen it in Toronto. It was a visitation not an imitation. Professionals, magistrates and doctors alongside the ordinary man and woman in the pew - all were affected.

Come and get it!

My altar call that morning was the most profound ever. With one leg raised in the air and hanging on to the pulpit for support, I was hardly a good advertisement as I challenged the people: "If you want this come and get it!" The response was amazing; everyone came to the front and we were there until 3 pm, a hungry and thirsty people.

Our very refined and sophisticated elder, Nick Hiscott, had to be carried to his car. Our other elder, Jim Elliott, who never danced or expressed emotion, was shaking like a leaf. The children fell to the floor as the Holy Spirit began to move powerfully among them. Every member was crying and professing their love for each other and, more importantly, their love for the Lord.

We had such a wonderful time we decided to come back that evening. And then the following evening. It was never my intention that Sunderland should become a renewal centre, but while God was there we wanted to be there, too, since we didn't know how long all of this was going to last. We came back night after night after night.

Meetings have now been held every evening except

Mondays for over a year, with thousands of Christians coming to us from all over Britain and the world – many returning again and again. Lives have been dramatically transformed, and many pastors, some of whom had been on the brink of giving up the ministry, have been re-charged with heavenly power following dynamic encounters with God.

Denominational barriers have come crashing down, with Anglicans, Baptists, Brethren and many others attending and helping with the meetings. Whether coincidentally or not, the city's sky-high car crime rate is down in the first half of 1995, and the local tourist board are in their seventh heaven: business is booming and the guest houses are full as people flock to renewal meetings. The grimy north-east image is changing. Meanwhile, the local church congregation has more than doubled from about 250 to 550 and we have already outgrown our new premises built only three-and-a-half years ago – we are now planning to move to a larger centre. At the same time we have planted two more churches in the area.

A foundation of love

However, just as the church in Toronto seemed to have been prepared for the outpouring, with a ministry team trained and ready to go, we had also been trained in love, service and sacrifice. Through trauma and tragedy we had built the church on a foundation of love, unity and caring for one, another based on the principle of John 13:35 where Jesus said: "By this all men will know that you are my disciples, if you love one another." We were in it together, our people were ready and willing to support us in all that God was telling us to do.

Sunderland has a rich spiritual heritage – it was one of the key sources of the 20th century Pentecostal movement and we had always believed God for a similar revival right from the outset. Many prophecies were given to confirm this. We were also strongly encouraged and stimulated to faith through friendships with anointed Christian leaders like Ray Bevan, Benny and Suzanne Hinn, Reinhard Bonnke, Suzette Hattingh, Wes Richards and Oliver Raper.

There was also the element of sacrifice. A number of people in our church, including ourselves, sold their houses and moved down-market in order to raise the cash for the building where the renewal meetings are now held. Brides-to-be gave up their savings and Suzette was moved publicly to give all she had.

Prayer has also been a vital factor. Influenced mainly by Suzette, who leads the intercession for Reinhard Bonnke's worldwide ministry, our church has placed a strong emphasis on prayer and spiritual warfare. We have often run all-night meetings attended by the bulk of the church, sometimes with their children asleep on the floor beside them. But the most important factor is that although we are the most ordinary of people, we have the most extraordinary God. Many nights in prayer meetings we sang the song:

> An army of ordinary people
> A kingdom where love is the key
> A city, a light to the nations
> Heirs of the promise are we...[1]

It became our theme song.

[1] Extract taken from the song 'An Army of Ordinary People' by Dave Bilbrough. Copyright © 1983 Kingsway's Thankyou Music, PO Box 75, Eastbourne, East Sussex, BN23 6NT, UK. Used by kind permission of Kingsway's Thankyou Music.

Chapter 2

Forgiveness becomes a lifestyle

I was brought up in the Assemblies of God as a third generation Pentecostal. Born in June 1955 at Barley Mow, near Chester-le-Street, I attended Birtley AOG until the age of seventeen, when my mother, concerned for my spiritual development, took me to Bethshan, Newcastle, where there was a large youth group. A few months after my arrival I gave my life to Christ.

The first time I ever saw my wife she was singing in the youth choir. But even though she was also a lively member of the youth group, I was soon to learn that as the only child of the pastor she had real problems with the ministry and her own relationship with the Lord.

We were married in June of 1976 when we were both twenty-one. I was absolutely convinced that this was the wife God had purposed for me, yet in the days that lay ahead that conviction was sorely tested as Lois was going through major adjustments in her relationship with her parents and her overview of church life.

Up to that point she had lived her life around the expectations of others and the unrealistic demands of good behaviour expected by some church members, which at that time seemed to hinge upon the externals of our Christian walk and not on the inner workings of the heart.

The quality I have come to know and love which sums my wife up best is her openness and refusal to be unreal. She had to be herself and not be judged by how many meetings she attended or what she wore. Teenagers often rebel but when you're the pastor's daughter it becomes a very public rebellion. On top of this, not everyone loves or agrees with the pastor, and when she heard the inevitable criticisms of her father her spirit was hurt and wounded. She determined she would never marry a man who had anything to do with the ministry.

Through all the searching and sifting at this time my wife had a real and life-changing revelation of the Lord. God kept us together, for which I am immeasurably grateful.

Secure in the safety of being a fingerprint officer's wife and a comfortable attender at church, Lois was apprehensive when the leadership at Bethshan asked me to take care of a small housegroup south of the River Tyne. She did not like small groups. Intimacy with people, who may expect her to perform as a leader's wife or who may reject her or myself, was not something she was willing to endure. She had a degree and was teaching English and Life and Social Skills at Gateshead College. She was very self-satisfied and kept her distance! Perhaps she should tell it in her own words.

Lois's Story

"I felt very inadequate and didn't want to say or do anything that would draw attention to myself. I hated anything that put me in the public eye and was unwilling to take any of the criticism that inevitably comes with being in leadership. If Ken was about to embark on a life of ministry he definitely needed a better-equipped wife. I was convinced I wasn't good enough.

"Like so many pastors' wives I struggled with the hurt and difficulties of my husband's ministry and so often compared myself unfavourably with others. I had unreal expectations of myself. My husband, I was sure, needed a wife who was a wonderful counsellor, teacher, super-duper homemaker and abounding with love and energy.

The ministry is lonely

"I also feared that my husband would give himself to God just as my father had done, and I did not want to be alone again. The ministry is lonely; I wanted somebody to be there just for me and not have to share him with God. I hadn't learned that truly the greatest joy is in 'adapting' myself, as the amplified Bible expresses it, to my husband, and to enjoy the intimacy of a shared life of dedication to the service of the Lord. I was not prepared to pay the price that everyone in God's service must inevitably pay.

"What made matters worse was that I felt physically inferior as a result of a serious fall when I was eleven years old. I was climbing in the garden on a rope and fell heavily on to crazy-paving. It provoked a condition which delayed the hardening of the bones in my spinal column, and throughout the next five years I had to wear a huge metal spinal brace. Each morning I was strapped into it, and every evening, with the help of my mother, I removed it from my chafed and bleeding limbs. I remember wanting to run from the taunts and stares of my peers at school. This deeply affected me as a teenager and left me scarred emotionally. I was angry that God didn't heal me, and resentment had become my stronghold. As a result of this I used to be totally overcome with fear whenever I was in a public place, church group or university class-room – anywhere I had to sit with other people.

"Then I met Pauline Harthern and it changed my life. She was the first Christian woman I had ever met who wore make-up, looked glamorous and yet loved God passionately.

"Pauline taught me the truth of forgiveness during time she took out to pray for me at the AOG Home Missions Conference in 1979. As she led me in a prayer of forgiveness for everyone I felt had ever hurt me, I understood for the first time the scripture: '*If* you will forgive, then your heavenly Father will forgive you'. 'If' means choice – the promise comes with the decision and is based not on an emotional feeling but an act of the will. So often we wait for the emotion of forgiveness when God asks us to choose to forgive. Suddenly I was free and am still free today. I love to sit on the front row and amongst any group of people."

Principles of kingdom living

In the meantime my father-in-law was going through his own crisis. Schooled as a very rigid one-man-band leader, he had come to the end of his own strength. An amazing divine encounter in Israel with teenage friend Roy Harthern, who was then the pastor of the 7,000-strong Calvary Assembly in Orlando, Florida, led to a revolution in his style of ministry and, indeed, his life.

Although a man passionate for God and single-minded in his pursuit of souls, Herbert had remained aloof from his congregation. But now he became aware of the tremendous importance of working at relationships in his own family and the unity of the body of Christ. This does not come easily and has to be worked at with a determination from all sides. The heart of it all was care for one another, which had to be applied both in the church and in individual families, ensuring that real love was the basis of the church's existence. It was upon these principles of kingdom living brought to Bethshan by Herbert Harrison that we have built our church in Sunderland.

Pentecostals have traditionally focused on ministry; what you do for God rather than who you are for God, and for us the externals had become a legalistic form. Instead we discovered that God looks upon the hidden issues and motivations of the heart, and not necessarily our outward presentation, and this began a revolution into reality.

It was into this setting that Lois and I began leading that first care group, building on the principles being absorbed into the larger church body. That care group spawned many others and soon God would call me into the ministry, but leading up to that call life was to take on some strange shifts.

Chapter 3

Police move blocked

Now that God had put purpose and love for him in our hearts, we wanted to get more involved in all that was happening in our church, Bethshan, in Newcastle-upon-Tyne.

It was certainly an exciting time to be there. The worship was vibrant and alive, there was rapid growth in the congregation and the unity was staggering. We felt sure that in order to be effective God would have us move nearer to the church; it was easy to feel like a 'dismembered member' living fifteen miles away.

My job in the Police Force restricted me to living within the borders of County Durham, and to move nearer our church would involve a transfer to the Northumbria Police. There was no reason why I should be turned down, and everything seemed to suggest I would be accepted. So, full of confidence and zeal for the Lord, we put our house on the market.

Two weeks later we were even more certain it was a good move when a first-time buyer purchased our property. Within a matter of weeks we had sold our home and were living with a family from our church.

The day of my interview dawned bright and clear and I

THE SUNDERLAND REFRESHING

went along full of confidence, but it was the toughest grilling I've ever had. They didn't want me! I was totally devastated. What made the situation worse was that now I would also have upset my Durham Constabulary bosses, who would be aware of my plans to move and who had invested a great deal of money in my training.

But into all the confusion came a word from the Lord brought by my father-in-law, Herbert: "Ken," he said, "I have a sense in my spirit that what is happening to you is for a purpose. God is going to do something about this whole situation and he will take you right into the centre of his will."

Promotion!

The next day my boss called me into his office, and with embarrassment I explained to him that Northumbria Police had refused to take me. I was staggered at his response. "Good!" he said. "I have two vacancies out of town for Community Police Officers in Ouston: one of them is yours." Ouston was as near to Newcastle as he could possibly give me and, because of the nature of the job, I was in effect being offered promotion!

But we still needed a home. One day casually walking through a shopping precinct in Newcastle city centre, we came across a property shop owned by a local builder and found a home in Ouston for sale. It was at a knockdown price, came complete with a mortgage subsidy and was ready for occupation.

Lois and her mother went to look at the house and rang me full of excitement. We qualified for the mortgage subsidy since, with no home to sell, we were technically first-time buyers. Convinced that God was in it we told the agent: "We'll have it."

28

It was twelve miles away from Sunderland and yet God birthed the present-day church from that very home. On the day we left, five years later, my wife and I stood in the lounge and remembered with tears running down our faces the wonderful blessing of God we had known in that house which the Master had chosen for us. Many, many people had come to know Jesus there, and we had known only incredible blessing, extravagant love and miraculous growth.

The church was about to be birthed.

Chapter 4

One hundred per cent

Amazingly, considering the love, unity and maturity of our people, the church in Sunderland is just eight years old. We began as a Sunday evening outreach from the 700-strong Bethshan church in Newcastle.

Herbert was a pioneer in Pentecostal circles in the sense of his willingness to learn from those in other groups. He was always open to embrace all that God was doing without necessarily taking on board all that he saw. 'Eat the fish and spit out the bones' was always his advice. I have since discovered that this openness to the whole body of Christ is one of the major keys to blessing and anointing.

And so it was that Bethshan members found themselves at the Dales Bible Week, which took place at the Great Yorkshire Show ground in Harrogate each August. It was run by the Harvestime movement, now known as Covenant Ministries, led by Bryn Jones. They were one of the new breed of 'house church' groups which emerged from the charismatic renewal of the 1970's, in which the practice of the gifts of the Spirit came to be more widely accepted among non-Pentecostals. There were accusations of 'sheep stealing' and 'heavy shepherding', but in fact many were attracted by the sparkling nature of the 'new wine'.

Dancing in the aisles

Dales became very popular in the early 1980's, with thousands flocking there from around the country each year to set up camp in the grounds and get a taste of the inspired teaching and worship. The worship profoundly touched those of us who had travelled to the Bible Week from the North East of England. A stream of beautiful new songs was sung with a passion and vitality that lifted people into realms of worship they had never known. It was a clean break from the stiff formalism so many of us had experienced, even in Pentecostal circles. We were used to clapping and raising our hands, but now dancing in the aisles became the norm. We discovered the truth of the psalmist's words, 'Where the Spirit of the Lord is, there is liberty'. (Interestingly, at the present time, beautiful songs are emerging from the pen of such men as David Ruis, Andy Park and Kevin Prosch and others. 'There's a Wind a'Blowing', 'The River is Here' and 'Light the Fire Again' are just some of the inspired songs emerging from this present renewal of God's Church.)

Herbert knew there was something in it for Bethshan. He liked the freshness of the movement and the worship, combined with the prophetic edge of the men involved, and it was at the Dales in 1982 that I received my call into the ministry under the anointed preaching of Terry Virgo who, incidentally, is at the forefront of this new move of God.

My whole family were camping for the week when one particular night I went into the big barn where the meetings were held with a friend, Syd Niven, from Alnwick, and about six thousand others. The moment we sat down a strange thing began to happen. I found myself weeping without being able to stop. Syd is a very sensitive man, and yet he looked at me and then totally ignored me for the rest of the evening. I asked him afterwards why he had done this and he told me: "I saw God was dealing with you and so I left you alone."

The walls are down

As the worship began I cried all the more and during the announcements I was more than embarrassed because, of course, no-one else was crying. The more I tried to control the tears, the worse I became. Soon Terry Virgo rose to preach – his theme was Nehemiah and he said: "The walls are down, the gates are burning and nobody cares. And because nobody cares God can't find a man in the city. But he knows there's someone." In a moment I knew why I was crying. The walls of our cities and our nation were down, and God was making sure that in me he could find a man who did care. The news that Jerusalem was in ruins devastated Nehemiah, and he went into prayer and fasting, even though he was miles away in Susa. And God was saying: "Ken, in you I've found a man that cares. Will you repair the walls?"

The Lord was breaking my heart and melting it, and as Terry was bringing his word to a close he determined to do something that he had planned for the following evening: make an appeal. "If this applies to you tonight," he said, "and you are determined to build the walls that are down and restore the gates that have been burned, whether in another country or in your own back yard, stand to your feet."

Instantly I was on my feet without knowing how I had achieved it, completely broken, totally devastated and sobbing from the pit of my stomach. As I lifted up my heart to God I prayed: "Father, tonight I am giving you one hundred per cent of my life." I became aware that I had always held part of myself back from a full commitment in the past. "If you feel you can use me," I told the Lord, "I give you everything I've got." It wasn't much. I had no Bible school training and I had never preached, but when I returned to my tent that night I knew that I had been called into the ministry. Uncertain of how I would ever be able to preach the gospel, shy and never an eloquent speaker, I was comforted by the words God spoke to Moses: "I will be with your mouth and teach you what to say." (Exodus 4:12).

The call of God

Travelling back home in the car, I told Lois of my experience and said I was ready to go anywhere and do anything for the Lord: would she go with me? I would have gone to the farthest corners of the earth, but deep in my heart I knew I had to build the wall in my own back yard. And even though Lois vowed to support me, she was to have some great struggles with the call of God on my life.

We came away with a determination to make a one hundred per cent commitment to God and the vision he deposited in our hearts, and that resolve has never left us. It became the foundation of our ministry and that is why people were later prepared to give up their houses, their savings, their time and their energy to join with us in this kind of dedication. Even today, in the midst of the renewal that has engulfed our church, our people give and give again in their service to God. Night after night they still give one hundred per cent in their commitment to all he asks them to do.

Soon after my return from the Dales, I was given charge of the remnant of a care group south of the River Tyne. This was a core of just four people, apart from ourselves. Who could have dreamed of what was just around the corner...

Chapter 5

The Dales Six

One year later Syd Niven and I once again sat down in the barn at the Dales Bible Week, along with 6,000 other worshippers. God was about to miraculously and supernaturally intervene yet again in the story of Sunderland Christian Centre.

Since we had some time to wait before the service began, Syd struck up a conversation with the people sitting immediately to his left. I watched aimlessly as his neighbour scribbled on a piece of paper, and then leaned forward to push the scrap into my hand. As the first strains of the opening song began to echo through the building, Syd whispered in my ear that on the piece of paper were the names of six people meeting in Houghton le Spring (a little town near Sunderland), all of them looking for somewhere to fellowship. Incredibly, these six people became the pillars of the developing work in Sunderland and they are still with us today! Without their unreserved service and enthusiastic support, the church could not have grown as it has.

Mick and Lil McGill, Frank and Elaine Talbot and John and Diane Crammen were originally brought together through the Billy Graham Prayer Triplet Scheme (the evangelist held a major crusade at Roker Park in Sunderland in 1984), and they began to pray continuously for a New Testament Church that was not a 'one man band' operation.

Overwhelmed by love

Soon afterwards, attracted by a Christian car sticker whilst on holiday, Mick and Lil met a couple from Wakefield, who passed on their address to Syd on that memorable evening. Lil had been badly hurt in their previous fellowship and was extremely reluctant to join or be affiliated with any other church group. So when she received my telephone call inviting her to our care group in Ouston, she was far from enthusiastic. However, God had his purpose in mind. After attending the group and being overwhelmed by the love of the people, little by little their barriers came down. Mick became a pillar of the church, as he regularly transported all the P.A. equipment from his home to the various rented premises we used in the early days. It was back-breaking and unseen work, but he was committed to the vision. Now he is regularly sent on missionary trips to Albania and, sensitively, with the same faithfulness, he serves on our ministry team.

As soon as we began meeting regularly with the 'Dales Six', our hearts were joined in a remarkable and supernatural way. However, in the continual development of our relationships, we have found love, commitment and forgiveness to be the keys.

Throughout the past ten years issues have had to be worked through, but we are bound together more tightly than ever before by the cords of love that encircle our whole church. Walking in that love, it is our greatest service to give it away night after night as people visit us from all over the world.

During the year of 1984 we began to experience phenomenal growth within our care group, and numbers grew from six to around 75 within eighteen months, by which time we had established five new groups. When Lois and I reflect on these exciting and foundational times, one of the key revelations God gave us then was how often relationships in the body of Christ were superficial. It became clear that we were hiding behind our spiritual jargon and practised veneer, failing miserably to be real with God and with each other. Gradually we removed our masks, confessed our weaknesses one to another and found that as we revealed ourselves to God and to each other, rather than being rejected, we were loved all the more! Now that we are seeing a similar expansion of rapid growth, it is our intention to plan another series of teaching on the 'Kingdom Living' principle upon which the church was built.

I struggled with shyness

Being leader of the group was, for me, a particularly difficult obstacle to overcome. From being a young boy, my struggle had always been with overwhelming shyness. Conversation was extremely difficult for me. The people who were present in Ouston in those days share with me the knowledge that for most of the evening I was unable to do anything more than sit quietly, struggling to find the right words to say, yet not knowing how to express them. Tongue-tied and embarrassed, I was profoundly aware of my own weakness. It is regrettable that we have brought the world's value system into the church, where we view those on the platform as having achieved a level of excellence which justifies their gift and anointing. The truth is that God *does* choose the foolish things to confound the wise – there are no 'superstars' in his kingdom.

From the oasis of that care group grew a unique love between us: we were an amalgam of people drawn together by the Lord, and our foundations were love, unity and one hundred per cent commitment to what the Lord asked us to do. The challenge to our hearts would repeatedly come: "Will you give God all that you are and go all the way in service for him?" Those foundations have equipped us well for today when the people of Sunderland Christian Centre, out of love for the Lord Jesus Christ, serve tirelessly, night after night, the strangers visiting their church.

A supernatural initiative

Quite sovereignly, we had groups of people from the same areas coming to us, although they were unknown to each other. At the time someone likened it to a train arriving at a station – as one group of people got off, another group of people got on to journey to the next stop. It seemed to be a supernatural initiative by God enabling us to easily plant new groups in their own areas, and from Ouston, care groups were established in Rowlands Gill, Washington, Hetton-le-Hole, Hebburn, Cleadon, Sunderland. Six in all.

At this point, Bethshan Church invited me to become Area Leader, looking after all of those groups, bringing a united vision and purpose. During the service when hands were laid on me for that spiritual office, I received a prophecy that if I remained humble before God, then in the future I would be like a fruitful bough planted by a well with branches hanging over a wall.

Following the expansion of the care groups, it soon became clear that it was time to begin meeting as a congregation. But the question was, where?

Week after week we prayed for the Lord's direction in showing us the place where we needed to become established and put down roots. I myself wondered where it should be. The town of South Shields, Washington or one of the other towns south of the Tyne estuary?

Pentecostal mecca

Sunderland appeared to be out of the question. It was a Pentecostal mecca, where in 1907 revival had brought about the birth of the Pentecostal movement in Great Britain and spawned a great worldwide missionary enterprise. Smith Wigglesworth himself had come to Sunderland when All Saints Parish Church were holding nightly meetings during a move of God and had received the Holy Spirit in such a measure that a life-changing miracle healing ministry was birthed. And there were already three AOG churches in the town, so to us it was not a consideration, even though it was then Britain's largest town with some 300,000 inhabitants.

During the spring of 1985 Herbert Harrison had invited Bryn Jones of the Dales Churches up to Newcastle to preach in Bethshan. Following a tremendous service, when Bryn preached on the faith of Abraham, Lois and I were invited over for supper, where we began to talk with Bryn about our plans. One of the privileges Lois enjoyed and, since I joined the family, I have also enjoyed, was being exposed to the heart and spirit of some of the great men of God who have stayed in Herbert and Mary's home. Lois remembers hours in her childhood spent on the knee of the great Pentecostal pioneer, Willy Burton, and how enthused we were by our fellowship with David Wilkerson and many other giants in God.

All roads lead to Sunderland

Bryn's response to my deliberations surprised me. "Where is the football ground?" he asked and, "Where is the University? Where are the main industrial and shopping centres?" "Sunderland," I replied. "Then if all roads lead to Sunderland," he concluded, "that is where the church needs to be." And so we planned to establish our congregation in Sunderland, but not without some difficulty since the other AOG churches were, to some degree, quite understandably offended by the attitude of a young upstart riding into the town with all guns blazing!

In August 1985 we held an opening celebration service in Wearmouth Hall, Sunderland Polytechnic (now University). There we announced that from September we would begin Sunday evening services in the basement suite of Crowtree Leisure Centre. The following month, at the age of 30, I left the Police Force and was taken on to the staff of Bethshan Church as Youth Pastor and Area Leader south of the Tyne, holding together the Sunday night congregation in Sunderland, as well as the various care groups around the city. For six months I led the meetings and Herbert preached; then for the next six months Herbert threw me into the deep end and he led the meetings whilst I preached. For two years we effectively remained an outreach from Bethshan Church, Newcastle, into the City of Sunderland, until in September 1987 we began Sunday morning services and moved from being a congregation into a church and from the basement suite to the plush function room upstairs.

The Sunderland meetings took off from day one. They were alive, anointed, purposeful and exciting. There was a definite sense that we were not just aimlessly meeting, but that it was the start of something initiated in the heart of the Father.

Obstacles to overcome

Going to church was most unusual, having to pass the swimming pool, go through the turnstile and up the stairs, but once inside the function suite we were cocooned in our love for the Father and for each other. Even so, there were many obstacles to overcome. The function suite was adjacent to the bar, which opened half-an-hour before our services closed, and we had to compete with the clinking of glasses and the conversations of the 'regulars'. Many times they forgot to switch the intercom off and all sorts of messages would interrupt our services – "Would Mr Jones please come to reception and collect his daughter" would suddenly intrude into the middle of our worship. Bomb scares – common in England at the time – would send us scurrying into the street in the middle of the sermon, and one memorable occasion, when this very thing happened, was the first time we had invited a distinguished speaker. Colin Urquhart spent much of his evening with us stranded outside the centre on the cold pavement while the police checked again for any hidden device. We remember even today his graciousness towards us.

The other thing we had to compete with was the cleaners. If the Sunday morning services did not finish at 12.30pm prompt (and those of you who know me well would realise this is an impossibility!) they would march in with mops, buckets and polish at the ready, irrespective of the people sitting in church.

During that time many good men of God, like Colin Urquhart, Barney Coombes, Ray Bevan, Oliver Raper and Frank Houston of Australia, would drop in on us on a Sunday evening after speaking at Bethshan in the morning. Frank Houston, of the Assemblies of God church in Australia, prophesied that we would witness a great and unusual move of the Spirit and that we would see unprecedented deliverances in that future move. The songwriter, David Fellingham, prophesied that the cloud of God would come and Sunderland would see a great outpouring.

Lois and I were always aware of the great historical significance of our town and we were firmly convinced that God would visit us again. But before any of this, the church family had to face up to tragedy...

Chapter 6

Heartbreak strikes

I remember looking forward to Christmas 1986 with greater expectation than usual. Lois was about to give birth to our third baby - hopefully a boy to join two beautiful daughters. As we hung up stockings and distributed presents we included some for the new arrival under the tree.

Just a week before Christmas we had lain awake thinking of names for our baby, and as we felt sure it would be a son we decided on Matthew – Gift of God.

Twenty-four hours later Lois was in labour and an ambulance was taking her through the cold sleepy streets. This was going to be a very special Christmas! She now tells the story in her own words:

Lois's Story

"I can remember hearing Ken laughing in the corridor outside my room. My mother and father had joined him at the hospital – our third child and their third grandchild was on the way! They had no idea of the drama unfolding in the next room.

'You are going to have to be very brave,' the doctor told me as I lay on the bed in the delivery suite. He took hold of my hand. 'Lois, I'm afraid your baby has died, but you are going to have to try to deliver normally.' 'Who is going to tell my husband?' I asked, pulling the oxygen mask away from my face. 'The registrar,' replied the doctor.

"When the words came, Ken couldn't really take them in. He walked into the delivery suite and took hold of my hand. His anguish and concern for me was overwhelming, but there was nothing he could do – except pray."

Nowhere to hide

"We really wanted this baby. For me it provided the reason to live a normal sort of life for a few years. I was still struggling with the demands of the ministry and the call of God, and a baby would have meant I could have opted out of some of my responsibilities. Now it seemed as if God was stripping away every last place I had to hide.

"Ken just kept on holding my hand as I went through the delivery, but when the baby arrived he cried out, 'Oh no! It's a boy!' and slumped to the floor in tears. How could a baby so pink, so beautiful, be dead?

"The nurse wrapped Matthew up, just like a normal baby, and handed him to me. As I cradled that little boy in my arms and gazed into his tiny face it all seemed to be just so wrong. He had died because the placenta had come away from my womb. There was nothing physically wrong with him. He had suffocated in the place which should have sustained his life!

"'She's haemorrhaging, she's haemorrhaging!' shouted the midwife, and suddenly there was blood everywhere! The nurses ushered Ken into the corridor and began the battle to save my life. I had noticed my stomach moving in a strange way – it seems that my blood wouldn't clot and the situation was very serious. I remember being covered in blood – it was even in my hair – and I was terrified. It was then that I made a vow to God: 'If you spare my life and restore me, I promise I will never opt out and hide away again. I'll do whatever you ask me to do and give one hundred per cent to the ministry.' I could have died that night, but somehow they managed to stop the bleeding. As I lay drifting in and out of consciousness, apparently I was asking for my mother. She was well known for her strong faith stance, and up to this point I had not been comfortable with it. But now I had no choice. While my own faith was weak, I had confidence in hers. She came and prayed for me, and slowly I began to recover.

"Yet through it all a scripture from the Amplified Bible was turning over and over in my mind: 'I have given you power over all the power that the enemy possesses, and physical and mental strength and ability so that nothing shall in any way harm you.'

Funeral service

"After a few days in hospital I was allowed home, and on Christmas Eve, a few of us – including Elaine, Di and Lil and both sets of grandparents – gathered in our small living room at Ouston for Matthew's funeral service.

"It was snowing by the time the undertaker lifted the small oak coffin out of the hearse. We walked behind as he led us to a little grave under an apple blossom tree in Birtley cemetery. Matthew was laid to rest on a cold bleak day, and I felt as if my heart was breaking.

"A few days later Ken stood in church and told our

people: 'There might be 101 reasons why it happened but, come what may, we are going to serve the Lord, and although we do not understand the whys and wherefores, we love the Lord more than we have ever done before!' His announcement had a profound effect on the congregation and caused the church to knit itself around us. We became very aware that little Matthew had caused us to become a family.

"Amazingly, however, none of these events took me completely by surprise. A week before our son died, I had seen it all in a dream – the hospital, the stillbirth, the dead baby in my arms. Yet strangely, in the dream, I remained pregnant and Ken and I walked together through a door into a huge harvest field. The dream was vivid, and it was to be fulfilled with uncanny precision, but it was another eight years before I understood just what the harvest field was all about.

"In the meantime, though, I was full of fear. Having lost my baby boy, I didn't want to lose my girls and husband as well. When you lose a child it can shake your faith in God's ability to protect your family, and I was afraid of all sorts of things, but didn't really know why."

Supernatural joy

"My feelings swung like a pendulum. On the one hand I had a supernatural joy – throughout that period I had the most incredible time of witnessing about the love of God. My doctor is part of the renewal now and a young woman who had also lost her baby came to the Lord. My midwife, who came to visit me on Christmas Day, heard me laughing and went back home saying, 'She is happier than I am and she has just lost a child'. She used to make excuses to come as she felt such a wonderful atmosphere in the home. She was so impressed that she wanted what we had and we led her to Jesus. But I also felt a deep grief, and I was aware that something deep inside me had been greatly shaken.

"I spent the next six months in and out of hospital in a very poor state of health. My whole life revolved around doctors, hospitals and high blood pressure – I was a complete physical wipeout.

I felt totally unable

"Ken, as well as having a church to run, had to do all the household chores. He did all the cooking, cleaning and ironing. But the spectre of the ministry loomed large, with the church growing apace. I wanted to serve the Lord with all my heart, but felt totally unable. The people in the church, meanwhile, just loved me and cared for me. They came and cooked for me and looked after me for two years. They kept us going.

"We sacrificed having any more children for the sake of the ministry. The specialist from the hospital where I had our girls said I could only have another child if I was hospitalised for my entire pregnancy. It's an awful feeling for someone who wanted a houseful of children – I was an only child, so choosing not to have any more was the biggest choice of my life. But the Lord told me that our spiritual children would be numerous. He said that my arms were empty now, but that he would fill them with spiritual babies.

"Physically, I was far from well, but I had come to an initial place of peace in my spirit. That place evaded Ken, however. He couldn't articulate what he was feeling and would get away alone into the bedroom and pray. He needed to find his solace in God.

"The last thing he needed was the arrival of an exuberant Welsh preacher."

Chapter 7

Fire falls at Frankfurt

Lois huddled angrily in our bedroom, sick and miserable, as a bold, big-hearted preacher persistently knocked at the door asking to borrow hair spray. Ray Bevan had arrived in Sunderland, and his strategic visit was again to provoke an amazing twist in the continuing development of the Sunderland story.

It was February 1987, only six weeks after Matthew's death, when Ray, who now leads the 1,200 strong King's Church in Newport (the fastest growing church in Britain), arrived in our home. He was an ex-rock singer working as an evangelist mainly in schools and, coming across one of his tapes, I had felt prompted to invite him to our church for a week of aggressive evangelism.

However, after the stillbirth of our son, it just seemed that this was the last thing we wanted to do. My wife was still sick in bed. We were both shattered and bemused, and for weeks I had tried to cancel his engagement with us, but he wouldn't take no for an answer. Much as he sympathised with us, he felt that he should come as God had told him to!

So it was that a fireball descended into our midst for

one week. Everywhere he went he spoke in tongues, even in the men's washroom of a local hotel – much to my embarrassment. He was excited, alive and full of something we most certainly did not have. And all the while he was with us he talked incessantly of a Fire Conference he had attended in Harare, Zimbabwe, the previous year, hosted by Reinhard Bonnke.

A life-changing experience

The primary purpose of this conference was to inspire evangelists and other Christian leaders and to set them on fire with the Holy Spirit so that their cities and nations might be won for Jesus. It certainly had been a life-changing experience for Ray, who still talks today about the lasting impact.

Ray was insistent that we should go to Frankfurt that summer for the first Eurofire Conference, but deep in his heart he was determined to reach out to my hurting, angry, isolated wife and lift her from her sickness and depression. His pretext of borrowing hair spray worked, and we will never forget how God used this challenging, yet obedient, man to change the direction of our lives – infecting us with a hunger for God which still drives us today. Ray's persuasion sent me to Frankfurt in the summer of 1987 for the Eurofire Conference.

How incredible the timing of God is. My wife's continuing ill health, plus the strain of the ministry had left me very vulnerable. Those who observe us today will be aware of the fact that we are very much a team. Neither of us is complete without the other, and the shock of nearly losing my wife, combined with her ill health, was very difficult for me personally. Since Lois had recently undergone unsuccessful surgery for a kidney stone and was awaiting re-admittance to hospital, she was unable to come to Frankfurt with me, and I left Sunderland with a heavy heart and a deep need.

Even though the airline upgraded me to first class, I was not able to appreciate the luxury of my journey. As I gazed out of the window and viewed the passing clouds, my heart ached and I bowed my head, my eyes spilling over with tears of despair. "Lord," I cried, "this is my last chance. If you do not meet me here, I am unable to continue in the ministry."

Following Ray's encounter I was looking for Reinhard Bonnke to lay hands on me and for God to give me a new release of anointing and purpose to go on. However, God was choosing to use another vessel to touch my life: Benny Hinn, leader of the 7,000-strong Orlando Christian Centre in Florida and, interestingly, Roy and Pauline Harthern's son-in-law. Again, I was gently reminded by the Lord that we so often judge men's ministries on their style and presentation and therefore miss the treasure God has for us through them. We need to consciously take judgement from our hearts so that we do not miss all that the Father has for us.

Slain in the Spirit

As Benny Hinn began to pray for us all in that large auditorium, God heard the cry of my heart. I was standing at the back, as far from the platform as I could possibly be, when at some point during the prayer I found myself flat on my back on the floor. I had never been 'slain in the Spirit' before and was the only one in my section of the crowd to fall. Eventually I opened my eyes to see interested faces peering down on me, wondering over the name on my badge – Gott – meaning God, in German!

On the last evening the praise and worship was electric. Reinhard preached a wonderful sermon and called the sick to the front for prayer. A 17-year-old girl carried her mother right from the back of the hall and laid her at the front of the platform. She was in the advanced stages of cancer and appeared just like skin and bone. Suddenly she caught Reinhard's eye and he looked at her and said, "Woman, you will not die, but you will live! When I pray for you, you will get up in Jesus's name!" He encouraged the congregation to pray in tongues and then, taking hold of her hand, he prayed, before hauling her to her feet and telling her to walk towards him. She took the first tottering step, then with each new step she took she became stronger. Then, throwing her arms up into the air, she began to run from one end of the platform to the other. Later, we heard that she had been healed and is now worshipping in a German church!

Suddenly God intervened

Following this miracle, the atmosphere in the fest-halle in Frankfurt was highly charged. Turning to Benny, Reinhard asked him to continue praying for the sick. So, taking off his jacket, he led the people right back into worship. Suddenly God was again about to intervene in the story of Sunderland and rescue the life and ministry of an insignificant and despairing young pastor!

Benny asked for all the English pastors to come up on the platform since he felt the Holy Spirit had asked him to pray for them. In that moment I decided I was going for prayer, whether or not I liked this man's style of ministry, and I literally ran to the front, jumping over seats to get there. I stood at the back of the crowd with my eyes closed when I heard a voice shout, "Young man! Are you an English pastor?"

"Yes," I replied. "Come here to me!" he said.

As I began walking towards him, I experienced one of the most unusual manifestations of the presence of God I have ever known! I can only describe it as like walking through a force field about one metre high. As he put his hands on me I crashed to the floor and became totally immersed in what felt like liquid anointing, and I found myself shaking and vibrating to such an extent that I later found that one of the cloths used to place over ladies' skirts was used to cover my chest as my shirt began to climb around my neck!

Never the same again!

From a distance I heard Benny's voice say, "Pick him up!" and I was hauled back to my feet. He prayed and blew on me, and once again I fell with what seemed to be electricity pulsating all over my body. "Pick him up again!" I heard him say, and this time he looked right into my eyes and said, "Young man, from this moment you will never be the same again!" And I wasn't!

I received a mighty impartation of the Holy Spirit that night. My preaching was different, I was excited and alive. I was filled with the joy of the Lord. My heart was enlarged, and I discovered a new, unqualified faith in God my Father. It was no longer a struggle for words when I met with my people. A power dimension had been added to the church. We were about to scale new heights of effectiveness in our church and God was to use two good friends to bring us to healing and health.

Chapter 8

Friendly intervention

_____

As God had used the Dales camp meetings previously to intervene miraculously in our lives and the life of our church, so God now began to use the Eurofire Conference in a similar way.

Even though I had returned from Frankfurt revolutionised, my wife had become increasingly sick and despairing. All the inadequacies she had felt in being a pastor's wife and an effective partner were being highlighted by her grief and ill health.

She spent most of her days in and out of hospital having her blood pressure – which could soar to alarming levels – investigated and kidney stones removed. Her whole life revolved around doctors, hospitals and high blood pressure. Her fear was compounded when, during a visit to the seaside town of Scarborough, she suffered a transitory attack, similar to a mild stroke, when a small blood clot moves through the brain without leaving any damage. It was a scary experience.

Whilst having a church to run, I attended to all the household chores, cooking, cleaning and ironing.

One of the positive results of Lois's hospitalisation was that she received an incredible compassion for the sick, never having been seriously ill in her life before. Some of the lives she touched affected her deeply. In the midst of our deepest distress, God was bringing some depth to our experience. We have been broken to pieces, but it is only in the brokenness that light can shine through. Because she felt totally lacking in confidence in being a pastor's wife, Lois became convinced that in her sickness God wanted to take her home, so that someone more effective could help me run the church.

If she won't come, make her!

Into this situation stepped Suzette Hattingh, during the prayer preparation for Eurofire, Birmingham, in 1988. Suzette came to stay with Lois's parents Herbert and Mary whilst conducting services in Bethshan, Newcastle. During the 'leaders and wives' meeting one evening, Suzette noticed that my wife wasn't with me and asked where she was. Having told her about our situation, she asked me to bring Lois to see her, and added, "If she won't come, put her in the car and make her!"

The next day found us sitting in Herbert and Mary's lounge, where Suzette bluntly asked Lois, "Did it really hurt when you lost your baby son?"

I could see that my wife was quite offended at what seemed to be such a ridiculous question, but haltingly she replied, "It broke my heart." Suzette responded by gently explaining that God was wanting to bring to birth something of the supernatural in her life and ministry, and that every time she aborted his plans for her life, she grieved his heart, just as her heart was grieving now for her baby. She emphasised the fact that God did not make mistakes, and when the nation of Israel sank into debauchery and sin, God chose insignificant little Hannah to bring to birth Samuel, the saviour of the nation!

Hannah was goaded and ridiculed by her rival Peninnah, and that afternoon we came to understand the Peninnah in our lives. Interestingly, Peninnah means pearl, and those things which grate and grind us are often the things which produce treasure in our lives. The key to the story of Hannah, as expressed by Suzette, was in the verse where it records "Hannah stood up", suggesting that she stood up on the inside as well as the outside, determined to change her situation.

So many of us have sat down and passively let things come at us and sweep over us when God is calling us to rise up and, using the power at our disposal through Jesus Christ and his cross, allow him to change our circumstances.

A son of vision

Samuel was the 'son of vision, prophecy, power and promise' and he turned the nation around. Suzette challenged Lois that day, telling her that God had sent her half way around the world to encourage her to be like Hannah, and to rise from her self-pity and bring a prophetic vision to birth through prayer. Finally she laid hands on her and prayed that God would strengthen and anoint her.

Lois was free at last! From that meeting she grew in strength day by day, and her ministry was increased as she began to see through new eyes. Suzette became a firm friend and an integral part in the development of the Sunderland story. Prayer became the central focus of our church, and through it we entered a new realm of power and effectiveness. To participate in prayer is the most exciting thing there is in the kingdom of God. The Father has chosen us to work with him, through prayer, in the advancement of his kingdom. Prayer is crucial; it can sometimes mean the difference between life and death.

Woken in the night

One evening Lois felt compelled to pray and lead others in praying for those who felt suicidal. At that very moment, one of our members, a nurse working in the casualty department of South Shields District General Hospital, was leading a young man to the Lord. He had just attempted to take his life. How many times have you woken in the night and wondered why you are awake? Perhaps it is that God is giving you a burden to pray through!

During her recovery, the Lord also spoke to Lois about the importance of being a godly wife. Although Solomon was judged to be the wisest man who ever lived, he was led astray because of his wives and, through him, the whole nation of Israel. She saw what a terrible effect Jezebel had on King Ahab. The 'wife' in Proverbs 31 paints a picture of a godly woman, strong in every area of her life, rising up early to glean spiritual food for her family. Her husband's success lay in her hands, and my wife began to absorb herself in the word of God, praying many hours day after day, gaining physical, emotional and spiritual strength, functioning in anointing alongside me. In the prophecy of Joel we are reminded that God has a great work for women as he pours out his Spirit in these last days.

Suzette believes that revival is only able to come when the members of the body of Christ are so revived that they

60

go and act on what has been renewed in their own hearts, reaching out for the lost.

Jesus Christ hung on a cross for a lost world, and the moment we take our focus away from the fact that this is still the heartbeat of God, we lose our own cutting edge.

The whole burden of her heart is that the body of Christ will so fall in love with Jesus that the love of God will drive us to seek the lost. She told me recently that the beauty of what is happening at the moment in the UK is that Christians are waking up to the fact that every one of them has to be used by God and that it is not just superstars and big men, but it is faceless people and everyday men and women who are going to bring in the nations. That will start revival!

The devil knows that a united church has the power to do anything in God. We Christians have been too busy fighting one another, and the church of Jesus Christ has been bleeding to death. But now the Spirit of God is here. We must stop arguing and love one another. If we do, the anointing will be so great it will shake the nation. God wants to change this country and he wants to change the church, but first he wants to change you and me!

Different strengths

Suzette's visit led Lois to take her place alongside me in ministry, and now we function with joy together on the platform. We always feel incomplete without one another! Lois is incredibly spontaneous, but my strength can follow through her initiative. She often picks up what the Holy Spirit would like to do, and then God enables me to carry it through. We have different strengths and weaknesses by which we complement each other, and by destroying my wife, the devil would effectively have been destroying me too!

The other key friendship which impacted our lives also began at the Eurofire Conference in Birmingham in 1988. Mary, my mother-in-law, decided that since she had received so much from the conference in Germany the previous year, she would offer to serve others by welcoming guests in the foyer of the Metropole Hotel.

Her job only lasted two hours, for within that time Benny Hinn and his wife Suzanne walked in, along with Pauline Harthern, who had played such a great part in both the development of Mary and Herbert's church and our own lives. They persuaded Mary to phone us and ask if we would like to join them that evening for dinner.

Never wanting to push myself forward, and also feeling a little bit intimidated, I was reluctant at first. Then Lois made me realise that if God was in this invitation I could miss his purposes for our lives. I never want to miss anything in God, so we agreed to join them.

Suzanne and Lois became good friends, and she has been a great inspiration to us both since that time. In 1989 she prophesied to a leadership group in Sunderland that people were going to travel from all over the world to see and experience what God was doing in our church.

Intimate experience

To witness Benny and Suzanne Hinn away from the platform encouraged Lois and I, more than anything else, to get to know God in a deeper way than we had ever done before. Benny's devotional life with the Lord is fundamental to all he does. His intimate experience with the Holy Spirit is more than just a platform reiteration. I have silently observed over the years that as he spends hours alone with the Lord, refusing to involve himself with newspapers, magazines and the mundane distractions of daily life, he is truly living a life of sacrifice and intimacy with the Father. He speaks often of 'dying to the flesh' and 'being willing to pay the price of carrying the anointing.' Away from the crowds and the cameras, I have seen a man who pursues God with all his heart and it has profoundly touched mine. Both Benny and his wife Suzanne, quietly and without any recognition, are incredibly generous.

Many times, during worship, he has led us into the very throne room of the Lord. It was my privilege, on one occasion, to sit with him in his bedroom whilst he wrote the draft of the first chapter of his book, 'Good Morning, Holy Spirit' and once he deeply challenged me by saying that God was looking for men in our nation who would break the mould, believe God for big things and bring the nation into revival.

When Benny came to preach in our church in Sunderland, he prophesied that God would double the congregation within a period of six months, and that is exactly what the Lord did during the first six months of renewal!

Both Suzette and Suzanne have had a large input into Lois's life, and they have crossed continents to get away together and pray with each other.

Soon many of us were to experience first hand what it meant to catch a glimpse of the heavenly realm...

Chapter 9

Angels step in

Lois could hardly believe her ears. What was it she was hearing? As she gazed upon 100 or so people standing before her in that Saturday evening prayer meeting, she was aware from their expressions that they were hearing the same thing – angels singing!

Lois has been leading the prayer ministry in our church since the time Suzette had dramatically intervened in our lives. Nearly the whole church turned out to pray every Saturday evening in the YMCA in Toward Road, where in years gone by Moody, Sankey and Stephen Jeffries have held powerful campaigns. When D L Moody visited the town in 1873, Robert Boyd of Chicago, wrote: "When I got to the YMCA, I found the room on fire. The young men were speaking in tongues and prophesying."[1]

Every Saturday night my once-timid little wife, who had resented any form of public ministry, now relished leading the people into prayer and worship. Through the fight for her own health God had taught her principles of spiritual warfare that would help her lead the church to fight for others.

Our people have always been very loving and supportive towards Lois, and because she was leading the prayer the vast majority came to give her support and encouragement. I am certain that the unity in those meetings was one of the factors that enabled the church to glimpse into the heavenly realms as it did.

One memorable evening some six months after we began the prayer meetings, everyone was involved in praying passionately for abused, neglected and hurting children, when suddenly we were silenced by a deafening roar of voices. Most of us fearfully thought that there was a large football crowd gathered outside the building, but the roar of voices was soon followed by drums, cymbals and musical instruments.

Awe and amazement

As we began to enter into worship we were aware of thousands of voices joining in and enveloping us in their melody. In awe and amazement we all stopped to listen, and our elder, Jim Elliott, down-to-earth as usual, stepped forward to see what could possibly be happening. It was obvious that no-one in the room was singing and yet there was a multitude of voices worshipping in the Spirit in glorious harmony. It was the most beautiful singing we had ever heard, incredibly high and with many harmonies. At that point a wind began to blow through the building. We could find no draughts or any other human explanation for it.

Interestingly, as my wife led the Ladies Conference in September 1994, a rushing mighty wind was heard by all the ladies present. It swept right across the building and then swept right back across the room again.

We didn't talk too much about the angelic singing publicly in the church because the whole experience was so awesome we did not want to defile it in any way. Week after week we experienced the same phenomenon. Indeed, even in the building in which we meet today, on more than one occasion during prayer meetings, we have heard angelic singing. Lois felt in her heart not to make too great an issue of the experience, but just to join in whatever it was the Lord was doing. We didn't want people to come seeking angelic experiences, but come to seek the face of the Lord.

During the past year, time and time again, children and adults alike have come forward to testify to seeing visible angelic manifestations during services. And this is not the first time that Sunderland has witnessed unusual events in the spiritual realm. Some reports of the 1907 revival witness similar angelic singing, while more outlandish meetings are also on record.

Crying out to God

Prayer was the major emphasis in our church at that time. Often more than 200 of us would pack into a room and pray all night: parents would bring children armed with sleeping bags and snacks. The worship was wonderful, and it was not unusual for men and women to fall prostrate on the floor, repenting and crying out to God to touch our city and nation.

News of our prayer meetings spread, and soon Lois was being asked to go and lead intercession in other churches. On these occasions the whole prayer meeting – at least 100 people – would travel to wherever the prayer teaching and intercession was taking place to support both Lois and the pastor and church involved. Wherever the services were taking place, a convoy would set off; sometimes 73 miles away to Haltwhistle, at other times to Newcastle, sometimes to Morpeth, Billingham and North

Shields. We were beginning to learn how to serve the body of Christ with the blessing God had brought to, us just as we are doing today.

As the pastors of Sunderland Christian Centre, it is a privilege to serve the precious people God has given us. Their love, support and encouragement has amazed us time and time again. Together we always believed God would once again visit Sunderland, but he had some big surprises for us on the way...

[1] Michael Harper, The 20th Century Pentecostal Revival, Hodder and Stoughton, London, 1965 Pages 25 & 26.

Chapter 10

Breaking down barriers

Whilst our young church was still growing apace, there was a continuing division in our relationship with some of the Assemblies of God churches in the city. Our own church was independent, but obviously we were still linked with the AOG through Bethshan Church in Newcastle, and there was an underlying strain between us. There was clearly some resentment on their part, while no doubt there was arrogance on mine.

We wanted revival, but God's hands were tied since there was division in the body. The Lord said that the world would know we were truly his disciples when we loved one another.

Argentinian evangelist Ed Silvoso, at the forefront of revival in his own country, says on this subject: "All the time we do not deal with broken relationships, we are dabbling with the demonic. The Biblical command is for us to be reconciled with one another, person to person, family to family, country to country."

One day I was sitting in my office when the telephone rang. It was Clyde Young, a man we considered to be a statesman in Pentecostal circles. He had pastored one of the AOG churches in the city for many years and, along with his wife Jean, had a powerful and supernatural anointing.

Clyde asked if Lois and I would like to go over for coffee. "What now?" I wondered as I drove around to Pastor Young's home, nervous about the coming encounter.

It was through this man's ministry that my own family had become Christians; in fact, my grandmother was his first convert, and my wife had received the baptism in the Holy Spirit as he laid hands upon her.

Generosity of spirit

When I got to his house, I found another AOG pastor and his wife there with us in the small sitting room. I was sure I was in big trouble, but what followed was one of the most amazing episodes of reconciliation I have ever experienced in my life. It taught me early on in my ministry a valuable lesson, as I watched a great man of God speak with a humility and generosity of spirit which was incredible to behold.

The whole purpose of that meeting was to ask our forgiveness so that we might be able to flow together and accomplish whatever God had in mind for the city.

"Can you forgive a foolish old man?" Mr Young asked, and I wept at the measure of his spirit. "Can you forgive an arrogant insensitive young man?" I replied, and with this we put our arms around each other, weeping as we prayed.

Within a week I took steps to join the AOG. This was an important breakthrough in the spiritual realm and now, night after night, we are seeing churches, ministries and leaders of every hue and denomination, not only in a committed and loving relationship with each other, but working together and sharing their combined resources for the kingdom.

God is breaking down our dividing walls. Baptist, Brethren, Pentecostal, Anglican, House Church, Methodists: we all worship, serve the Lord and minister together. One of the greatest joys of this move of God upon our lives has been both the restoration and initiation of relationships right across the body of Christ.

Since that memorable morning, Lois and I have been prompted to visit Clyde and Jean on other occasions, simply to ask that they may lay hands on us and impart some of the treasure within them. It is so easy to look at a thriving blessed church community and forget the years of digging, watering, praying and toiling that previous saints of God have done in preparation for our reaping. Sunderland has known generations of godly men and women who have dug and toiled over the ground. We are now privileged to be reaping. Clyde and Jean Young are such people, and the Sunderland story would be incomplete without them.

Now we were about to learn the cost of our vision...

Chapter 11

A living sacrifice

───────────────

"Oh no, Ken," Lois said determinedly. "God would never ask us to give up our lovely home to build the church right now; we cannot move." After months of seeking God and searching for a place to worship, the Lord clearly began speaking to the leadership team concerning our church, building programme.

We had been spilling out into the aisles at the YMCA, but with a great many of our members being unemployed, students and young couples, the prospect of putting up a building did not seem possible.

It appeared to be a good idea at the time to follow the American model of holding multiple services. So we began meeting at 9 am and 11 am, and following the 11 am service we would all jump into cars and travel to Morpeth, where we held an afternoon service as we helped out in a new church plant.

Needless to say, it was a lesson all we pastors learn at some time or another: never initiate something because it seems like a good idea; only begin after prayer and confirmation from the Lord. I nearly killed the people and almost killed myself; we weren't ready for it, and I had to repent of having made the wrong decision and leading the church into something that was not on God's agenda. What works for one does not necessarily work for another, and unless God gives you grace for a specific task, it will not succeed.

So, after much prayer, we decided to look for a place of worship. We viewed an old run-down cinema, a Kawasaki motorcycle shop and even approached the council for land on which to build. It all came to nothing, but here we were, once again, about to witness God's miraculous intervention in our story.

One balmy evening

One balmy summer evening, one of our care group leaders held an outreach barbecue in his large and pleasant back garden. After good food, good fellowship and singing, I gave a short gospel message. Right there in the garden the Lord wonderfully saved a whole family, who were to be more than influential in the days that lay ahead.

The father of the family was a quantity surveyor for the local authority who, hearing of our search for a plot of land on which to build, decided to help us. He came to me one day with a map showing three pieces of land on offer, all in the east end of town, and as I looked at one plot, I just knew it was the right one. It was nice and square, nearest to the town and the largest. It was also a stone's throw away from the old AOG church building now known as the exchange building.

The quantity surveyor miraculously drawn by the Lord guided us through the whole of our church-building programme.

God had again supplied someone essential for the development of the vision.

74

Design and build

One evening the leaders met, and after prayer we decided on a 'design and build' project, which was cheaper. The builder's architect submitted a design, along with a tender. The design we chose (interestingly the cheapest) was originally planned to be constructed in two phases, beginning with a 400-seater hall, later to be converted to a 600-800 seater.

Lois had been reading of Alexander Boddy, the vicar who led the Sunderland revival in 1907 and was challenged to build a large parish hall that was soon filled with people from all over the world, who came to seek the baptism in the Holy Spirit. Since my wife was convinced that the same would happen again, she encouraged us to decide on building stage one and two together. Thank God we did. During John and Carol Arnott's visit to our church last October we actually seated 1,200 in the auditorium, although we have been restricted by fire regulations since.

Time spent on my knees

The cost for such a project was initially £500,000. It was a mammoth task for such a relatively poor congregation, and I often lifted my heart to the Lord and asked how we could generate this kind of money. After much time spent on my knees, I knew we should not go ahead until we had raised the £100,000 cash deposit ourselves.

As I reflected upon this, I thought of how we could raise it. I knew we had no-one in the church who could give £500,000. Nor did we have two who could give £250,000 or four who could give £125,000. In this way I kept breaking down the figure, but when I reached fifty I did wonder whether we had fifty families who could raise £10,000 each.

At our eldership meeting that evening, before I even had chance to say a word, Jim Elliott announced that after praying about it he felt that God had given him a strategy for raising the money. He explained that he had been wondering: had we anyone who could give £500,000? Had we anyone who could give £250,000? Had we anyone would could give £125,000? But then he felt God had said to him, "No, but I believe there are fifty who could give £10,000". As he spoke my jaw dropped in utter amazement, and I knew then that God was speaking.

Leading by example

That night the five of us each committed ourselves to giving in that way. For most of us it would mean selling our homes and raising the money on the equity, and as I explained the strategy to our people, we led them by example. As to my own wife, her initial reluctance to leave our home with its pretty leaded windows, country-style kitchen and fantastic garden changed after hearing clearly from the Lord, and she was more enthusiastic than us all. God had spoken to her from Haggai chapter one, about the people of God living in panelled houses whilst the church of God was in ruins.

Later Lois and I felt that the Lord may be asking us to give everything, and in fact we did move down market three more times into smaller homes. However, our joy was full and we were very blessed as a family.

Last year we asked the Lord for a miracle, and with very little capital we were able to buy the lovely home we now live in. On April 30th 1994 we moved in, and only months later all heaven broke loose. With all that that means in terms of disruption to our lives, we knew that God had provided this house for us.

Exposure to the faith of great men who have had big visions, has encouraged me to believe God for big things. So the church began a time of great sacrifice, and we all gave what we had.

Giving everything

John and Diane Crammen, two of the church's original 'Dales Six', were typical of the many families in the Sunderland church who gave everything to pursue the vision. Diane's nickname used to be 'Margo' after the character played by Penelope Keith in the television series 'The Good Life'. Her fulfilment came from her beautiful home and she did not like anyone dropping in, either for coffee or to eat, who might disrupt the line of her rug, or the symmetry of her furniture. The only way they could release money was to move, and Diane was challenged by the Lord about the idol of her perfect home.

As the sign went up in their garden, an amazing change was to be brought about in her heart.

The quantity surveyor who was so valuable in guiding our building programme through, had a large Victorian terrace house divided into bed-sitting rooms in a very run-down area of the town. He was selling this house in order to raise money himself for the project. It was dilapidated and run-down, had no central heating, needed rewiring and had graffiti all over the walls. Worse still, the neighbours were alcoholics, male strippers and prostitutes, yet the moment John and Diane walked through the doors they knew it was the right house for them and that

God wanted them to live amongst these people. They sold their home, bought the terraced house and lived in it just as it was for two years, releasing two sums of £10,000 towards the project.

Now, in their beautiful 'done up' home, people come from all over the world to stay with them in their quest for more of God in the renewal, and the Government has pumped hundreds of thousands of pounds into the reconstruction of their street, so raising the value of their once-squalid property. The whole area has been physically and spiritually lifted, and God has proved to us all once again that you can never out-give him. It has cost John and Diane thousands of pounds to re-fit every room, but miraculously the money has always been supplied.

Other couples who gave sacrificially received their investment back within months. Suzette Hattingh herself went the whole hog and gave her life-savings to the project.

Widows gave their all

Within a short time we raised the £100,000 and decided to go ahead with the project. Supernaturally the congregation just kept giving and giving over and over again, with none of us really knowing where the money had come from. We never received a grant or large gift from outside of the fellowship. Widows gave their all to help pay for chairs, and even my own children laid a sheet out on the pavement and raised £55 by selling their toys.

We never missed a deadline for paying the contractors, though we were often right up against it. We would have a bill to meet by Monday morning and would simply pray the money in. On one Sunday morning £12,000 came in the offering – and that was over and above the normal giving to the church. On another occasion I handed over a £20,000 cheque just five minutes before the deadline. God was teaching us about faith, and we were being stretched at every level. Having raised more than £350,000 ourselves, we are now left with a £200,000 mortgage.

'Lord bring your blessing to this place'

Work began in the spring of 1991, and the shell took six months to build. I remember Suzette standing in the vast auditorium and praying, "Lord bring your blessing to this place." We fitted out the shell over the winter months, with our own tradesmen in the church working long and hard, and the building was officially opened on the 29th March 1992.

However, we weren't just bothered about bricks and mortar. Evangelism went hand-in-hand with everything we did and we were always looking for ways of reaching the lost. We sampled the Willow Creek model in the year leading up to the renewal. This was a tried and tested principle practised at a large church just outside Chicago, in which services were adapted to suit the culture of those you were trying to reach.

So we would give the Sunday evenings over to this kind of meeting, which was more like a gospel concert in form, with minimal audience participation. It would be focused around an interview with a leading personality, who would be drawn on how he or she found Christ, and this would be used as bait to catch the fish.

But we knew that despite all our evangelistic efforts we were not making much of an impact on the tens of thousands of needy people around us. We desperately needed rain from heaven to ripen the harvest.

Little did we know, but there was already a cloud on the horizon...

Chapter 12

Holy fun down at the font

"Ken – what do you think about flying down to London early tomorrow morning? A few of us from the church are going over to Holy Trinity, Brompton..."

A key factor in all of what followed was my relationship with Wesley Richards, the senior pastor of the King's Church in Slough, right in the shadow of Windsor Castle. Wes and I were old friends, and we'd both seen the importance of relationship. We also saw the need of 'networking' and breaking the north-south divide. We have long felt cut off here in the north of England. We always had to go somewhere else – usually south – for meetings and conferences. Now they're having to find out how to get to Sunderland! The local tourist board love it!

Our friendship came about through Herbert Harrison's relationship with Wes's father, Billy Richards. And it was out of this relationship that the Lord spoke to Wes, saying: "When you go to HTB (Holy Trinity, Brompton) invite Ken Gott as well."

He has told me since that he resisted this prompting on two occasions, but the third time it happened he felt compelled to phone me, having made an agreement that we would include each other in whatever we were doing.

Wes had just returned from a trip to Spain when he heard about a meeting at HTB, which was being held specifically for church leaders. He couldn't even tell me what the meeting was about, other than that it was probably something to do with the Toronto Blessing. And it was taking place the very next day – 300 miles away in London!

Holy Trinity, Brompton

I had heard that there were some things happening at Holy Trinity, Brompton, but all the same it seemed a long way to travel for a meeting. "Listen Wes," I stalled, "I'll have to check a few things first and then I'll call you back." I put the phone down.

"Ken – I really feel you should go," Lois said when I told her about the invitation. I knew the flight would be quite expensive, and I felt I couldn't justify spending over £200 just to meet up with Wes and visit an Anglican Church in the middle of London. Then I remembered the £100 I had been given a few days earlier in church. The donor was convinced I would be making a trip to Toronto and said he wanted to help me on my way. I tell you, no such trip was in my mind!

Lois rang to see if he objected to his money going towards a visit to Holy Trinity, Brompton, instead. He was delighted because he, too, had heard about how God was moving down in London. The next obstacle was the airline; Lois rang to find there was just one seat left. Perhaps God was in this after all.

Once I got there, however, I wasn't quite so sure. Our party of five sat near the back, and while I had somehow imagined there would be 400-600 people present, there were only about 130. There was no great buzz of excitement or sense of expectation. Everyone seemed very laid back, and they all talked with plums in their mouths. It was all a bit too posh for an ex-bobby from the north!

Then the vicar, Sandy Millar, welcomed everyone. He was almost apologetic as he said: "We'll start with a time of worship, if that's all right." Fancy asking permission to start the worship! I found myself wondering what on earth Anglicans could teach me, a Pentecostal, about the Holy Spirit. Also their church paraphernalia, the stained glass windows, baptismal font and altar all made me feel uncomfortable. Then a gentleman got up with a guitar and started to play Vineyard music. Until this point I had never thought much of Vineyard music, feeling it to be sentimental, but then God began to touch my heart and I felt his presence.

Glued to our seats

Bishop David Pytches, Vicar of St Andrew's, Chorleywood, and a former missionary to South America, started to explain some of the phenomena associated with the Toronto Blessing. Then the ministry time was announced. We didn't surge forward, but stood observing towards the back.

Then God spoke to me very clearly. He said I had forgotten how to drink from other spiritual 'wells' and that I needed to drink from the 'well' at HTB. At that point, one of Wes's team nudged me in the ribs saying, "I think we need to humble ourselves and go and ask the Bishop to pray for us." Things were starting to happen around us. Some people were falling to the ground, others were laughing, some were jumping up and down. We walked down to the front of the church.

A divine thunderbolt

Wes asked Bishop Pytches to pray for us. "We want all that is on offer," he said. The Bishop began to pray: "Thank you for these men. But they want more of you. So Holy Spirit – come and get them!" At which point we were all struck by what seemed to be a divine thunderbolt and fell to the floor. Then we started to laugh. I was rolling first one way then the other, holding my sides which were aching with laughter. I had rolled under the baptismal font, and every time I looked up and saw it I laughed even louder. Infant baptism was not part of my tradition, yet nothing seemed to matter. God was doing something very mighty, and he could do it however, whenever and wherever he wanted. At one point Bishop Pytches walked across and stood over me. He sealed me with the sign of the cross and I thought, "Hmm, this is nice...I like it." He was totally unpentecostal in his approach, yet his prayers were powerful. The more I laughed, the more I felt the burden of the ministry lift from me. God was freeing me up on the inside and it was amazing.

Reckless for God

Then a woman came across. I heard her amused observation: "Look at the state of these men here," but I didn't care – my pride had disappeared through the stained glass windows! Then she started to slap us on the chest, praying: "God, make them reckless for you." And we all shouted in unison "Yes!"

Suddenly we were like fish in the water and we were swimming in all this as if we were made for it. The transformation was unbelievable.

Lois, meanwhile, was cooking lunch at home in Houghton-le-Spring when the phone rang. I was calling her from my mobile in Hyde Park. We were howling with laughter and must have sounded completely mad.

Not too exciting!

We went back to HTB for the prayer meeting that night. It was an unspectacular service, but when the ministry time came the Holy Spirit came in power all over again.

I had a lot to think about on the plane coming back home. God was at work and he didn't care about people's labels. I knew I was lighter in my spirit. The pressure I'd been carrying and the strain of it all was off. It was as if the Lord had taken the load. I knew that he had much more for me and that somehow Wes's invitation to HTB had been very significant.

On returning, Lois asked me to pray for her. She took the next Sunday morning service as I was away preaching. She preached about having pure motives so that the Holy Spirit could move in power, and after giving an altar call it seemed as if most of the church came to the front. Many fell on the floor laughing and one man shouted out: "Jesus, Son of David, have mercy on me!" There was much repentance with weeping.

On the Sunday evening I returned to a special meeting to share with the church my experience at HTB – we had been having a break from our Sunday at Six, Willow Creek-style, services for the month of August. We listened to a tape of Ellie Mumford's visit to Toronto, which is now widely available and was recorded at HTB on May 29, 1994. Ellie, who is the wife of John, pastor of the South West London Vineyard Church, simply shared about her visit and the wonderful fruit she had seen.

Agony of soul

Afterwards we prayed. About 100 folk were there, and hilarious laughter broke out affecting some of the most unlikely people – one woman, a magistrate, was almost under her chair laughing. Many people were deeply touched.

The next day we left as planned, for a summer holiday we had booked in Scotland, but we got no peace while we were away!

Numerous phone calls from our staff persuaded us that we should visit Toronto. God was plainly doing something in the world, and it had exploded in our church. We could only imagine what would happen if we went to Toronto for a whole week!

We were both amazed and humbled by the response of the people at SCC (Sunderland Christian Centre). They had been so pleased and excited with all that had happened, they gave a freewill offering to send us to Canada which came to £3,500 in all. It was far more than we needed, so when we boarded the plane James, our youth leader, was with us.

Shortly before we left Suzette phoned us from Toronto. She and Gayle Lemon, her co-worker, were on their way to Brazil and managed to find time to fit in a visit en route. We still had some reservations, but she put our minds at rest. "I've been all around the world, and in all kinds of revival situations," she said, "but I've never felt the presence of the Lord like I have here – and something wonderful has happened to me!"

We had no idea what God was going to accomplish in and through us during our visit and neither did the people back home...

Chapter 13

God's interventions

Let me take a little time to break into the narrative here and reflect on the implications of God's intervention in our lives.

I never dreamed what the repercussions of that one phone call from Wes Richards would be upon my life and the life of my church. As I sat in the Dales Bible Week and heard Terry Virgo speak on Nehemiah, I never dreamed that what seemed to be another ordinary meeting would turn out to be a life-changing experience.

Who could have guessed that the visit of a dynamic Welsh singer would spin our lives in another direction? All of them were life-changing experiences, after which I was never the same again. God was taking the initiative.

The Bible is littered with similar accounts of his intervention in the lives of men and women as they routinely plodded through their daily lives. Moses, at the burning bush, Gideon on the threshing floor, the list goes on and on.

Elisha was in a rut in more ways than one! There he was in 1 Kings 19 ploughing a field: up and down, up and down, up and down. Meanwhile, the one God was about to use to break into his life, the prophet Elijah, was in the wrong place doing the wrong thing, finding himself there because he believed a lie.

Elijah had believed that the army of God was no more than a load of dead prophetic corpses, and that he alone was the only one left. Worse than that, he believed that very soon he, too, would be a dead prophetic corpse! He should have known his God could not be defeated and that he would not allow the prophetic voice of the nation to be wiped out.

In obedience to the Lord's command, Elijah returned on his way and anointed Elisha as prophet in his place. He found him ploughing: up and down, up and down; a mundane, uneventful day, and yet unknown to him it was going to be a day that would change his life forever. God intervened and in an instant Elisha's life took on a new direction.

In Acts chapter 10 we read of another divine intervention. This time God spoke into the life of the Apostle Peter which changed his own personal direction and, more importantly, the direction of the early church.

Up to this point the church had been going along quite nicely, when here we see God miraculously alter the apostle's plans. The church was a few years old, and Peter had been preaching the gospel to the circumcision only: God had to break in to completely annihilate his plans for an exclusively Jewish church.

Thank God for the times when *he* takes the initiative, not man. It is very comforting to know that this present move of God did not have its origins in a deacons' meeting!

In verse 10 we see Peter experiencing a very powerful manifestation. God puts him into a trance, following which a sheet descends from heaven and through the events that unfold God clearly shows Peter that it is his will to save both Jews and Gentiles.

But in verse 14 we see Peter respond to God with the words "Not so, Lord." He didn't reply in this way as a deliberate act of rebellion, but he could not conceive of God asking him to do such a thing. Nevertheless, through the vision Peter's heart was convinced. The gospel was about to be preached to the Gentiles.

As God intervenes in our lives, he is looking for a positive response in our hearts – a resounding "Yes" to what he is doing. Thank God that this Holy Spirit initiative, this move of God, was accepted by the other apostles. They changed and adapted, and today there are countless millions saved as a result. We need to be open and expectant for God's interventions in our lives.

Had I not accepted that invitation from Wes, all the wonderful things that we are experiencing now may never have occurred.

And I was about to experience more!

Chapter 14

The Toronto Blessing

Like many other curious visitors, we checked into the budget Monte Carlo Hotel – just down the road from the Toronto Airport Vineyard's building.

Queues of people built up early for the evening meetings, which had been held nightly since the 'fire fell' on 20 January 1994.

While we were far away from home, we soon discovered we were not among strangers. As we 'jammed' in with 450 others, we found ourselves sitting next to my old friend Syd Niven, who had been with me at the Dales.

We had not seen him for years, and yet here he was again about to play an important part in the next phase of our church story. He had spotted us in the restaurant, discovered our room number and come knocking at our door.

As we sat together waiting for the service to begin he introduced us to Dave Roberts, editor of Alpha magazine, a popular Christian periodical in Britain, and we hit it off with him straight away. Dave was following John Arnott around researching for his book 'The Toronto Blessing'.

During the worship Dave tapped me on the shoulder and explained that John Arnott was waiting in the corridor and that he would like to meet us. As we left the auditorium we wondered again at the intervention of God in our lives.

We talked with John for some time about mutual friends and our church in Sunderland, and then before he left John simply asked if he could pray for us. What happened next was certainly outside our previous experience. Lois began to behave just a like a puppet on a string. She was bobbing up and down and shaking from head to foot. "Has your wife ever done anything like this before?" John asked. "Never," I could truthfully say. "Well Lord," he added, "just bless her and give her all the more." Suddenly – boom – she was laid out on the carpet. Having watched with astonishment what had happened to my wife I was rather apprehensive as he approached me.

My spirit was stretched

Unfortunately, I have always battled with being overly self-conscious and I was afraid of being publicly embarrassed, but John prayed for me and invited the Holy Spirit to come. Immediately I bent forward with my arms and legs outstretched and my fists clenched and it seemed like my insides were growing and growing and trying to burst out. I was aware of a stretching and enlarging of my spirit. Smith Wigglesworth described such an experience himself, saying he felt about ten times bigger on the inside than on the outside. I was reminded of the children's character The Incredible Hulk, growing and bursting out of his clothes.

Dave Roberts then prayed a prophetic prayer over me: "Lord, cause this man to light fires in the North of England."

Instantly I saw a vision. I had never experienced a

vision before, but this was extremely vivid and in it I saw a wilderness filled with desert bushes which one by one spontaneously burst into flame. Each one joined the other and soon they all merged into a huge blaze. I found myself shouting, "I can see it, I can see it!"

Gospel preacher Jean Darnall had a similar vision, in which she saw a fuse lighting up places all around Britain and eventually exploding in the North East.

Profoundly changed

As the vision subsided I fell backwards and began my time on the carpet. For a long while I felt my spirit being stretched. Then I heard John say, "Well, they seem to be having a good time; let's just leave them there." I do not know how long we lay there, but when we got up we had been profoundly changed by the Spirit of God.

Finally, we managed to pull ourselves together and returned to the auditorium, where the worship was still going on. Ian Langdown, one of our members, just happened to be there, too. He was on holiday in Florida when he quite spontaneously decided to fly up to Toronto. Now he's one of the leaders in the renewal.

By this time I was laughing my head off and Lois was telling me to 'Ssh!' but I just laughed and laughed. She was so embarrassed.

Ian was taking notes – he is senior lecturer in Mathematics at the University of Northumbria and is very precise.

All the time I was laughing, however, God was deeply chastening me about the manner in which I had led the church he had entrusted to me. At times I had been heavy-handed and had never really relinquished control to God. It was the beginning of a great change.

The next morning we found the worship to be deeply and profoundly moving. How gently the Lord deals with us. Testimonies followed, and John announced that Lois and I had come from the place where Smith Wigglesworth had been baptised in the Holy Spirit and where the Pentecostal movement had begun in Europe.

It burned up the debt

I told the congregation all about Sunderland's heritage, describing the plaque outside All Saints Parish Church hall in Monkwearmouth, which commemorates the Pentecostal outpouring of 1907 with the inscription: "When the fire of the Lord fell, it burned up the debt." I explained that I had come to Toronto with the same purpose as Alexander Boddy had visited Wales during the Welsh Revival when he went to see what God was doing, determined in his heart to bring it back to Sunderland. It has always been my desire that God would visit our city once again, and I was looking for a day when a new plaque would go up recording that the same thing had begun in 1994. We wanted God to visit Sunderland again! John Arnott turned to me and said: "Ken, as surely as you stand beside me today, revival will come to Sunderland."

We hit the floor with a bang and Lois and I were ministered to throughout the whole service. The dedication of Carol Arnott and the team who prayed for us for such a long time was one of the things that amazed us. Never before had we witnessed anyone praying with a selfless dedication for such a long time. This was certainly a model we would adopt upon returning to Sunderland.

I began to struggle, shake and fight on the floor, and during that time I felt the Lord release me from all the bondage of expectation and restriction I had felt in my ministry.

Meanwhile God was also dealing with Lois who, following Matthew's death, had a very real fear of death and separation from those whom she loved. Secretly she had a paralysing fear of hospitals and dental visits; doctors terrified her. That morning on the floor, God washed it all away as she, too, had an open vision: she saw the Lord. He was full of animated joy and love. Heaven was resounding with praise and there was dancing and celebration on the golden streets. She was absolutely enthralled by the joy of it all and knew in that moment with total certainty that death held no fear.

The streets that are golden

Within an hour, that which had tormented Lois for eight years had gone, and she was left wondering what she had been afraid of for all those years. Ever since, the song my wife has loved to sing over and over again is 'The Streets that are Golden' by David Ruis, in which he describes the joy of the glorious bride and the bridegroom on the streets of heaven.

Lying there on the carpet that Sunday morning, I told the Lord that I was no longer bothered about my dignity. We needed to be full of the Holy Spirit when we returned to England.

Lunchtime came and John and his wife Carol, who were leaving the next morning for church camp, invited us to lunch. Dave Roberts and James came, too. Later they took us back to their home and after sitting and chatting for only a few moments, they asked if they could pray for us some more.

As soon as John asked to pray for us I felt the Spirit of God descending all over me. It is a witness to their love and dedication, and their willingness to bless others, that although they must have been weary, they prayed for us all afternoon and into the early evening. Prophecies were coming thick and fast. Lois saw a hand being prized, finger by finger, from the church; the fingers on the hand represented the five-fold ministry gifts. God was taking control away from men and taking back his church.

Eventually I was through

Then I began to see a thick and thorny hedge all around me, and as I lay on the floor I realised I was trying to fight through it. In my spirit I knew that the hedge was all of the expectations people had of me which had become too great a burden to bear. It also represented the restrictions I placed upon myself as I tried to be the perfect pastor, never failing, never doing anything wrong and always saying the right thing. I realised that I was physically acting out what was taking place in my spirit and fighting through the things that had bound me up. Eventually I saw light and glory and knew that I was through.

Dave Roberts, who had been sitting there quietly, at this point began to prophesy. He had been wondering what I was going to do when I got through the hedge, and the moment he began to speak we knew that the wondering and waiting for the understanding of an eight-year-old dream was about to be fulfilled. "I see a mighty harvest field," he began, but before he could go any further Lois burst into tears and began to weep profusely. It was only that morning she had received her healing from the fear of death, and here was a man we had never met before prophesying the very thing she had seen in her dream one week prior to Matthew's death. A harvest field and the two of us walking into it together, with someone we did not know prophesying as we entered it.

We felt an immediate heart link with John and Carol Arnott, and out of that a friendship has developed between us. They are both broken vessels 'fit for the Master's use.' God has given us the security of knowing we can trust our lives to them. They will not speak a word against anybody, and they are always humble. Their hearts are only for the kingdom of God and not for any self-glorification. It would appear to be a day when the Lord is knitting hearts together quickly, giving an instant recognition of those to whom you are linked.

Our youth leader James had been receiving from God, too, although not in a demonstrative way. But we came into the 'movers and shakers' category – those who responded to the Spirit's presence in a very obvious way. Oddly enough, John doesn't manifest much himself, although he takes a great interest in the phenomena and causes pandemonium every time he prays for others.

Dramatically affected

Ian Langdown had sought God intensely all week, but found it very hard to receive. The Lord finally blew away all his religious expectations and filled him to overflowing in a sophisticated restaurant. He was so dramatically affected that he could hardly stand, his hair stood on end and he couldn't count his coins when he was paying his bill. Now when he preaches laughter often breaks out among the congregation.

Determined not to leave until we had received all that

God had for us, we asked James to try to get good seats for our last night. He waited for hours after being first in the queue and we sat right behind the seats reserved for the ministry team. In fact, throughout the week James was more interested in looking after us than in what he could get out of it, and we were deeply touched by his love.

Following John and Carol's departure, Randy Clark had taken over the ministry for the week, and on that particular evening he stopped the service after the opening songs saying he must obey the Holy Spirit. "All those who are senior pastors and have crossed an ocean to get here, come out to the front. God wants to impact you in a mighty way," he said. About forty of us surged forward – ten per cent of the congregation – including pastors from Australia. Randy then prayed and the power of God came upon us, knocking us to the floor. A wonderful sermon followed, expounding on Bartimaeus and the woman with the issue of blood and how they had pressed right through the crowd in their determination to receive healing from Jesus. We were pressing through to touch the Lord ourselves that night.

Noisy endorsement

We lay on the floor right through the sermon, and I noisily endorsed and encouraged the preacher in everything he was saying, repeating his points after him.

Lois, meanwhile, had fallen at the feet of a lady called Belma Vardy. Incredibly, Belma was looking for somewhere to stay in England while she taught on a dance course. She came back to England with us and was at the first nights of renewal in Sunderland, almost like a midwife at the birth of a baby.

As Lois lay surrounded by the love of God she was aware of a man leaning over praying for her. There was a wonderful communication of love and compassion oozing from him. He took hold of her hand and said: "No longer will you feel God's presence through the touch of man. The Lord will touch your life himself; he will hold your hand; you will become a friend of God and move into deeper realms of intercession."

No-one had been near her

Lois was incredibly moved by the whole essence of the man and turned her head to thank him. Astonishment gripped her as she realised she could not see him anywhere in her vicinity. Urgently, she asked the people sitting over her, one of whom was Belma Vardy, where he could possibly have gone. Tinged with a sense of awe, they haltingly explained that no-one had been anywhere near her. We leave that experience without explanation, but to say it was remarkable is most certainly an understatement.

During the ministry time I began to manifest deep groans – possibly something to do with the emphasis on intercession in our church. Then Janice Chevreau, wife of 'Catch the Fire' author Guy, prayed for us and the joy of the Lord hit us. I remember a young woman coming over – she took one look at us and burst into fits of laughter. All this went on for three hours and we were radically impacted that night.

Ready to go back to the hotel, we negotiated ourselves through the open door, and as Lois and James walked towards the car they realised I was no longer with them. As soon as the fresh air hit me, my legs caved in and there I was crawling, with difficulty, on my hands and knees, across the car park! Almost crying with laughter, they struggled to lift me into the car and James drove us to the hotel, where once again I crawled on my hands and knees across the car park, through the lobby, past the reception-ist and upstairs to our room!

The hotel was much used by visitors to the church and, apparently used to sights like this, the receptionist didn't even bat an eyelid!

We had soaked in the Spirit for seven days. There had been laughter, weeping, shakes and jerks, but the greatest work of all had been a deep repentance. We had a greater love and passion for the Lord Jesus Christ than we had ever experienced in our lives before. Lois and I were conscious of the physical presence of God and we never wanted it to leave us.

Sunderland, the birthplace of the Pentecostal move-ment in Europe, was about to receive fresh fire...

Chapter 15

A Well of Blessing

In the past great men of God have dug wells in Sunderland and the North East of England.

During the eighteenth century John Wesley regularly visited the region. In May 1742 he wrote: "At five, the hill on which I designed to preach was covered from top to bottom. I never saw so large a number of people together, either at Moorfields, or Kennington Common. The word of God which I set before them was: 'I will heal their backsliding, I will love them freely.' After preaching the poor people were ready to tread me underfoot, out of pure love and kindness."

And in June 1757 he declared: "I proclaimed the love of Christ to sinners in the market place at Morpeth. In the evening, I preached at Sunderland. I then met the society and told them plainly; none could stay with us, unless he would part with all sin, particularly robbing the king, selling or buying run goods, which I could no more suffer than robbing on the highway. This I enforced on every member the next day. A few would not promise to refrain so these I was forced to cut off. About 250 were of a better mind."[1]

Sunderland was also a focal point for the outbreak of the 20th century Pentecostal movement which has spread like wildfire round the world and which now encompasses some 300 million people. For much of what is happening now also took place at similar meetings in the early part of this century in a parish just across the river from SCC, led by an evangelical Anglican called Alexander Boddy.

Although remaining an Anglican, Boddy, too, became one of the key figures behind the Pentecostal movement. As a four-year-old in his cot he saw a vision of Jesus and his disciples. Yet despite this extraordinary beginning he got caught up in wild escapades as a young man, including a hair-brained canoe trip up the coast, from which he had to be rescued by some Sunderland fishermen. His spirit of adventure later took him to far-flung countries, but also no doubt provided an ideal channel for a new move of the Holy Spirit.

Snatched from death

He was once snatched from death – apparently through angelic intervention – as a runaway cart crashed into the bicycle he was riding. He suddenly found himself watching the accident from the other side of the road!

As it happened, his family were related to Methodist founder John Wesley through the French Huguenot Vazeilles.

He was appointed to the charge of All Saints in 1886, having previously served as a curate in a rural area near Durham. Churchgoing in his new parish had fallen drastically, with the former vicar's drink problem no doubt a contributing factor.

It was about this time that American evangelist D L Moody visited Sunderland. So many people turned out to hear him that the police were called and huge crowds had to be sent away. And it was here after a Moody visit that one of the early manifestations of prophesying and speaking in tongues occurred.

The famous preacher F B Meyer wrote of those humble beginnings: "I can see him now standing up to lead the first prayer meeting in a small, ill-lit room in York, little realising that it was the seed germ of a mighty harvest. It was the birth time of new conceptions of ministry, new methods of work, new inspirations and hopes."

Moody and Sankey and their families stayed in York for five weeks before passing on to Sunderland. Here their meetings were attended by many more. A better spirit was evident and much larger numbers professed conversion. The chapel in which their first meetings were held soon became too small for the audience, necessitating the use of one of the largest halls in the North of England.

The editor of the Newcastle Chronicle, a Mr Cowan, then a member of Parliament, wrote about the meetings in his paper, speaking of them as 'a wonderful religious phenomenon.' It was a very unusual thing for such a prominent secular paper to discuss religious matters, and Mr Cowan's article created a profound impression throughout England. Invitations to hold services began to pour in from all sides.

Holy confusion!

In May 1879 the Newcastle Chronicle also covered the story of an all-night Salvation Army meeting. The correspondent was not altogether sympathetic, but after describing the hall, the participants and the singing, he continued: "This chorus might have been sung perhaps a dozen times when there was a shrill scream, a bustle around the platform, and a general rise of the audience. Seats were mounted; hands were raised in the air; the singing was mingled with loud 'hallelujahs', bursts of vociferous prayer, shouting and hysterical laughter. To add to the confusion, four of the forms fell backwards and threw their occupants into the common heap on the floor. So great was the commotion in the centre of the room, so terrifying was the din, that this incident, which would have thrown an ordinary congregation into uproar, passed almost unnoticed. Sinners were creeping to the penitent form; the Salvation Army was rejoicing; fully one-third of those present acted as if they were more or less insane. Several figures were bent double near the platform, groaning and wringing their hands."

Passion for revival

So Vicar Boddy somehow, in the midst of caring for his flock and running the church's many activities which included weekly open-air meetings, found time to travel the world, visiting Russia, Egypt and the Holy Land among other places. However, it was his passion to see revival among his working class parishioners that drove him to seek God for a fresh outpouring of his Spirit.

Boddy himself was aware of a lack of power in his own life and message. In an age where Biblical Christianity was coming under increasing attack, he realised it needed more than words to draw a largely disillusioned populace back to church. So he and his congregation began praying – sometimes well into the night – for the baptism in the Holy Spirit and revival in the community.

Meanwhile he commissioned the building of a new parish hall to accommodate their expanding activities, and was sent by his parishioners to Wales in 1904 when revival broke out there. He stood alongside Evan Roberts, a preacher at the forefront of the move, and was awe-struck by what he saw as thousands came to Christ and whole communities were changed. According to Pentecostal pioneer Donald Gee, "When he recounted what he had personally seen in Wales, it stirred both pastor and people to yet more earnest prayer and expectation of great things from God."[2]

Boddy tried to get Roberts to come to Sunderland, but it never happened. However, he heard about a Cornish-born Norwegian preacher called T B Barratt, who had caught the fire of God at Azusa Street in Los Angeles in 1906 where the Pentecostal manifestations of tongues, healing and prophecy were very much in evidence. Interestingly, some reports have said it was called the Los Angeles Blessing at the time.

Barratt came over to Sunderland at the end of August 1907 and held meetings for several months. Hundreds of people came from all over the country to seek new power in their Christian lives.

Great blessing

In the early twentieth century Donald Gee in 'Wind and Flame' describes the events at that time: "People had been praying for many months that he would come. Early in September 1907 he attended a Saturday evening prayer meeting in the vestry of All Saints Church where there was reported to be 'great blessing'. The next day Pastor Barratt was asked to preach in All Saints Church immediately following the usual evening service conducted by the vicar. The service was followed by a prayer meeting when many received very marked blessings, and a few came through to a scriptural baptism of the Holy Ghost. The meeting continued to 4 am on Monday morning." The Pentecostal revival had commenced in the British Isles.

Meetings were then held in the large Parish Hall every afternoon and evening, with a waiting meeting in the vestry after each service that usually continued far into the early morning. Added to those who had previously gathered at Sunderland for these special meetings, there now began to come a steady stream from various sections of the Christian Church. The meetings grew continually, both in numbers and influence.

Divine providence

The daily newspapers were used by divine providence almost more than any other agency to bring the news of what was happening in Sunderland before the notice of multitudes who otherwise might never have heard. The extent of these reports probably justified Mr Barratt's words on September 13th, that: "The eyes of the religious millions are now fixed upon Sunderland."

When the Vicar's wife received the gift of the Spirit in a meeting that lasted until 1 am, she not only spoke clearly in tongues but sang most beautifully.

Sometimes those newly filled with the Spirit would go home through the empty streets in the small hours of the morning as outwardly intoxicated as those who had been drinking the wine of this world (compare Acts 2:13). But how different both the cause and the effect! In this case even their bodies were renewed, strengthened and filled with new life, while the aftermath was pure blessing.

Smith Wigglesworth, a plumber and lay preacher who, despite dire warnings from other Christians that what was happening in Sunderland was of the devil, had travelled up from Bradford. Disappointed because he did not speak in tongues after some days of intense seeking, he resolved to return home and called at the vicarage, where the Vicar's wife told him: "It's not tongues you need, but the baptism!"

Though he was convinced he had already received it, Mrs Boddy prayed for him and on October 28th 1907 the fire finally fell. He spoke in tongues and was a changed man. He wrote later: "On Sunday morning, October 26th, after waiting upon God, I went to the Salvation Army meeting, Roker Avenue. After praying, the glory of God covered me. I was conscious at the same time of much of the experience I believe Daniel had in his tenth chapter. After this I regained strength to kneel, and continued in the Holy Ghost glow all the day, still realising a mightier work to follow. I went to All Saints, to the Communion Service, and after this was led to wait in the Spirit; many things taking place in the waiting meetings continued to bring me to a hungry feeling for holy righteousness. At about 11 am on the Tuesday at All Saints Vicarage the fire fell and burned in me till the Holy Spirit revealed absolute purity before God. The glorious remembrance of those moments is beyond my expression to give – an irresistible power filled me – today I am actually living in the Acts of the Apostles' time."

Apostle of Faith

Wigglesworth went on to become a leading pioneer of the worldwide Pentecostal movement of which Assemblies of God is a part. And he made a profound impact for Christ in many lands, including the United States, South Africa and New Zealand, where he was a catalyst for revival. He was known as the Apostle of Faith and saw miraculous healings wherever he went, including the raising of at least 14 people from the dead. His influence was such that books about him – he never wrote or read any himself – keep coming off the presses. The change in him was reflected in his powerful preaching and no-one was more surprised than his wife, who had done all the speaking at their Boland Street mission until then.

Stanley Howard Frodsham, in his book 'Smith Wigglesworth: Apostle of Faith'[3], recounts what then took place in Smith's own words: "I was giving out the last hymn when the secretary of the mission stood up and said: 'I want what our leader has received.'

"The strange thing was that when he was about to sit down he missed his seat and went right down on the floor. In a short while there were eleven people right on the floor of that mission. The strangest thing was that they were all laughing in the Spirit and laughing at one another. The Lord had really turned again the captivity of Zion and the mouths of his children were being filled with laughter according to the word of the Lord in Psalm 126:1,2.

"That was the beginning of a great outpouring of the Spirit where hundreds received the baptism in the Holy Ghost and every one of them spoke in tongues as the Spirit of God gave utterance."

Laughter in the Spirit

Interestingly, Wigglesworth later referred to the laughter phenomenon during a sermon on the gifts of the Spirit in Wellington, New Zealand, in May 1922.

"It may seem very strange to some people," he told the congregation, "but I have seen people come into a meeting down and out, exhausted and the power of God has come on them with laughter. Laughter in the Holy Ghost brings you out of everything! It is a thing you cannot create. The Holy Ghost laughs through you. You laugh from the inside. The whole body is so full of the Spirit of life from above that you are altogether new. For God to come into a needy soul and create laughter within is very wonderful."

The happiest day of my life

Boddy meanwhile kept a cool head as he chaired the meetings with firmness and grace and answered his many critics without malice or anger. Some evangelicals, including Reader Harris, who had himself encouraged people to seek the Holy Spirit, labelled 'tongue-speaking' as satanic.

The Sunderland Echo of September 30th 1907 reported on the first tentative steps of what became a universal movement, describing it, according to the authors of a book on the subject[4], as "Like a baby, it was not at all sure of itself and quite amusing...helped along by a black preacher who was unable to stop himself from laughing!"

The Echo reported: "Suddenly a dark gentleman who had been sitting quietly at the side of the hall started a revival hymn which was sung with vigour by the congregation, many of whom were on their knees. The hymn ended and the dark gentleman began in fervent tones to ask that the Spirit of Christ might come into the hall. While so engaged he burst into loud shouts and instantly the bulk of those present broke into exclamations led by a gentleman with a powerful bass voice who repeatedly exclaimed 'He is here, he is here'.

"The dark gentleman continued to laugh strongly and said, 'I can't help doing it I am so happy. It's the happiest day I've had.' 'Hallelujah, hallelujah,' was shouted from all parts of the building. Ladies were burying their faces in their hands as they knelt at the forms and the excitement was intense."

At the same time there was a renewed emphasis on the blood of Jesus and many healings occurred at the Sunderland meetings, including that of a deaf mute. A pastor from Berlin was healed of cataracts.

Supreme importance

Sunderland hosted regular conventions in the years that followed, providing hot ammunition for men of every denomination to spread the pentecostal fire. Donald Gee in his book 'Wind and Flame' wrote: "From the point of view of the early history of the Pentecostal movement in the British Isles, the Sunderland Conventions must occupy the supreme place in importance."

"Whether he was teaching about the Bible, lecturing or writing, Boddy's outstanding ability to communicate in plain, simple English was one of his strong points," according to the above-mentioned book. "This striking directness came across in his everyday encounters and in his religious life. As a committed evangelical, he placed a primacy on faith despite the wonderful acts of healing, discernment and prophecy that he experienced. He appreciated that faith is the primary source of a relationship with the risen Lord Jesus, not...a reliance on emotional experiences."

Although his co-workers may not fully have realised it, the spreading of his literature played a vital part in establishing Pentecostalism – thousands of Boddy's pamphlets found their way into seekers' homes, even as far away as the USA.

Boddy would have preferred everyone to stay in their denominations and fan the flames of revival from within, but the Pentecostals were largely persecuted and felt forced into setting up their own structures.

The movement was spreading and would more than likely have taken off in a big way in Europe had it not been for the untimely intervention of World War I. Men's minds could only now focus on immediate survival and became largely distracted for decades to come from a genuine pursuit of God while the war also created social problems which another revival would need to deal with.

Boddy, meanwhile, used the parish hall as a convalescent home for wounded men and even visited Sunderland soldiers in the war zone! So much more could be said of the man. He helped the poor with food and clothing, dragged errant husbands from public houses, took children on trips to the seaside and was always handing out sweets.

Model parish

The seaside jaunts began with a couple of hymns and a short sermon, after which the children were given a bucket and spade. And it was there on the beaches of north Sunderland that Pentecostal converts were understood to have been baptised. All Saints was in so many ways a model parish, where love, support and compassion could be seen actively at work.

Though remaining in the Church of England, Boddy was effectively the prophet and guiding force of the fledgling Pentecostal movement – a man filled with the love of God who hungered for yet more.

Jesus said: "Blessed are those who hunger and thirst for righteousness, for they shall be filled." The current move can rightly be traced back to men like Boddy who acted upon these words of Christ. More than that, hundreds of millions of Pentecostal believers across the globe today are to some extent the fruit of one Sunderland pastor's faithfulness and prophetic vision.

The spiritual well dug in 1907 was about to be reopened.

[1] Wesley's Journal: published by London Isbister & Co Ltd
[2] Wind and Flame: Donald Gee – published by Assemblies of God Publishing
[3] Smith Wigglesworth, Apostle of Faith: Stanley Howard Frodsham – published by Assemblies of God Publishing
[4] Alexander Boddy: Pastor and Prophet, published by the Wearside Historic Churches Group for All Saints' PCC in 1986.

114

Chapter 16

Re-digging the well

There is no doubt that one of the major reasons we in Sunderland and other places all over the world are experiencing such blessing today is due to the fact that great spiritual giants of previous generations dug out a deep 'well' which God is again re-filling.

In Genesis 26 we read the account of Isaac re-digging the wells of his father Abraham: "Then Isaac dug again the wells of water which had been dug in the days of his father Abraham, for the Philistines had stopped them up after the death of Abraham; and he gave them the same names which his father had given them."(NKJ)

We have again found a well of living water which springs up, refreshing us and all who come to drink.

Our lovely church building, which we sacrificed so much to build, stands in the east end of Sunderland, near to the docks, one of the most deprived areas of the city. The structure is large and rectangular with an extremely high sloping roof, and able to comfortably seat between 600 and 800 people. When we decided to lay carpet over the whole floor space little did we realise what a wise decision that would turn out to be!

Surrounding the perimeter of the site is a seven-foot-high fence, overlooked by close circuit television. A professional firm of hired security guards in uniform patrol the grounds linked through radio receivers to the local police station.

All this is necessary to protect the vehicles of visitors to the church, since marauding gangs take pleasure in stealing and vandalising cars. The guards are very efficient; only once during the present refreshing did a German visitor park his car outside of our security system and was left with a vehicle so damaged it was no longer of any use. Feeling very sorry that a visitor to our country should be treated in such a way, we took up an offering to help him get home and purchase another car.

Good citizen award

The offering that night was £3,000 – far more than his old banger was worth! We were so glad to be able to help this precious brother in this way. Some time later we were amazed to find that because of this the local paper awarded us a good citizen award, which one of our elders received on behalf of the church from the Lord Mayor of Sunderland.

So suddenly was the life of our church turned upside down we have had to make major adjustments to our lifestyles, and outlooks.

Prior to August 1994 about 280 of us, very ordinary people, sat in the centre section of the church building on a Sunday morning believing that one day God would fill it. In fact, we all bought at least one or two extra chairs for those we expected to fill them. Never in our wildest dreams did we anticipate Australians, Dutch, French, Koreans, Brazilians and all the others who have come to fill them!

Although whilst on holiday to Florida in May of 1994 a

lady called Kathy Lechner, considered by many to have a tremendously accurate prophetic gift, prophesied over my wife. She said: "Go back and tell the man of God, that which he built is too small and I am taking him back to my drawing board, says the Lord, and I will bring them in in this latter-time harvest and revival, and they will look and marvel, and dignitaries will come to that place, and I will bring my servants from around the world and they will prophesy in that place." Quite amazing, in the light of what has happened since August 1994.

Many Sundays as we sat surrounded by empty space, seeing the stacked empty chairs alongside the wall, we tried by faith to imagine what the hall would look like filled to capacity.

How startling it was to find that happen almost overnight! Not only is the building filled with those coming to the renewal, but our own local church has multiplied to such an extent, we are hard-pressed to get everyone in.

Breakfast is later!

Our very settled church life has altered radically; instead of three services a week there are six evenings and one Sunday morning. We watch open-mouthed as coaches disgorge their passengers, sometimes two or three an evening at weekends. Lois and I fall into bed around 2 am most days, exhausted but thrilled by all that the Lord is doing. Breakfast is now much later in our household!

From a routine of producing a few letters and church bulletins every week, our office staff has tripled to accommodate phones incessantly ringing with inquiries about meetings, visitors descending at all times of the day and night, and thousands of letters to be distributed.

Of course, everyone stretches to the limits when between 2,500 and 3,000 people come to our conferences, of which we have held four in the last year. Members of the congregation take care of car parking, stewarding, hospitality registration and general servanthood. Lois and I are continually amazed at the commitment and love we see in our people, as well as the many other churches who are helping in this time of refreshing.

Front page news

We also have to deal with an ongoing interest from the press, most of which has been extremely positive. Television stations from home and abroad have often sent their cameras, while our local station produced a very good programme. The Lord has again put the church on to the front pages of the secular press.

On February 16th 1995, the Sunderland Echo produced a centre-page spread on all tha. was happening, beginning with these words: "Thousands of people from all over the world have swelled the congregation at Sunderland Christian Centre since the Toronto Blessing arrived. Yet until a few months ago this was simply a local church in the evangelical tradition. Now the centre has become a tourist attraction. Over the past few months thousands of people young and old have passed through this church from Europe, USA and Australia. Every night of the week except Monday there are services regularly attracting up to 600 people."

Following this article a special feature appeared the following evening declaring: "A Sunderland church is at the centre of a religious revival, but it's not the first time it has happened on Wearside.

"Scenes of religious fervour as described in last night's Echo are not new to the city, they last happened in 1907.

"Last September 1,200 people queued at Sunderland Christian Centre from 5 pm onwards for a special service. Did I hear a 'Praise the Lord' from Sunderland's hoteliers and seaside landladies?"

And a large northern paper reported our conference in April 1994: "In an area not noted for its soul, 2,500 born-again believers offered theirs to God. Drugs cannot give the young this kind of high."

One of the main insights we gained while lying on the carpet in Toronto was that God wanted us to give Sunderland Christian Centre back to him. We realised how our style and method of ministry had kept the control of the church strictly in the hands of the platform gifts, and we knew the Lord had challenged us to open up ministry to the whole body. We had been deeply touched and impressed by the service, sacrifice and selfless giving of the ministry team in Toronto, who had prayed over us hour after hour with humility and patience.

Unprecedented growth

After the initial Sunday morning service on our return when we publicly repented before our congregation and gave the church back to God, Sunderland Christian Centre has changed beyond all recognition. People who had warmed church seats for years are now playing an active part in the ministry. Prior to this move I had always struggled with the John Wimber model, feeling that ministry should be plat-form and pastor-centred, but God has burst in on my way of thinking and we are now seeing unprecedented growth in the hearts and lives of our people.

Most of our church members are on the ministry team, together with many from other churches and denominations. They come from all walks of life: House-wives, nurses, teachers and doctors; we have them all. Practical training has been given and definite guidelines have been laid down, but God is simply using their willingness to serve the hundreds who come night after night.

God is not looking for superstars or exceptionally talented people to swim in his river; rather he is search-ing out ordinary nobodies who become extraordinary somebodies when touched by his Spirit. To watch these 'nobodies' walk out from their seats and pray for people and then to observe as the Holy Spirit powerfully interacts in the lives of individuals has been one of our greatest joys.

Holy Ghost ministry

Nora and Doris, two of our more elderly (I must be careful here!), motherly and much loved ladies have come into their own. Looking after children, making tea, fussing young mothers and pampering the pastor have all had to be squeezed into a busy diary of Holy Ghost ministry! Doris, at the time of writing, is on an exhausting mission-ary trip to Albania, and Nora has seen people receive physical healing as she has laid hands on them and prayed for them. We cannot hold them back. Of course, they are only two of the many people serving God in a humble and refreshing ordinary way. While it has definitely been the most exciting time of our lives, it has also been the most exhausting.

Mind you, the renewal couldn't have been maintained

without the selfless support of the many other churches from all over the North-East, including Anglican, Baptist and Brethren assemblies, who are now sharing the burden of running the renewal meetings. This came about at a leaders' lunch in April – after we had been going non-stop for eight months.

Spontaneous support

The pressure had worn us out and we felt the only solution was to cut the renewal meetings down to three nights a week, certainly as far as our church was concerned. But, quite spontaneously, pastors and church leaders present came forward and their message was clear: the meetings had to continue and they and their churches were prepared to give whatever help was necessary. This meant they would provide a ministry team, worship leaders, musicians, stewards, someone to man the bookshop...and there were a host of other considerations. And while they may have different styles in their own churches, they would submit to our house rules and ethos. The response was amazing as pastor after pastor came to the front pledging their support. They felt it a privilege to be involved.

All this must be quite unique – and only God could have achieved it. As you can imagine, it requires complete trust on our part and unselfish service on theirs – but the love of God is being poured out in these days and there is no shortage of Christian generosity.

Considering that the first recorded crime in the Bible was the result of a dispute over the correct way to worship the Lord, this must be quite a miracle! No-one involved is looking at what they can get out of it; only at what they can give towards extending the kingdom of God. We realise that we're all in it together. This move is crossing every denominational barrier and is bringing the body of Christ together.

The huge demand for prayer and ministry each night has meant a clear need for people we knew and trusted to be available for this purpose on a nightly rota basis. And so 350 people came to ministry training days, and we now have a pool of over 300 spirit-filled believers from various churches and denominations with the same desire to humbly serve. These precious servants are called upon to regularly pray for people at the renewal services and conferences.

Toronto model

We also decided to model our renewal services on the way they were conducted in Toronto, with worship and testimonies followed by the word and ministry. Since we are not pursuing primarily the manifestations but the fruit of changed hearts and lives, we give time every evening for people to share what God has done in their lives.

You see, we need to know what we are about in these days. It's not simply jerks and shakes, laughter and tears; but we are plugging into a power source we have been devoid of for too long. The Lord is calling out to the hearts of men and women and saying, "I'll come again if you'll let me, in a way you have never known before, if you open up your hearts and spirits as you've never done before."

The early Pentecostals hungered for God with a determination and resolve we need today. They were willing to pay the price for that hunger. At times despised and rejected, they knew the only solution to the problems of their generation was the power of the Holy Spirit.

The formula hasn't changed. Peter stood up on the Day of Pentecost and said: "This is that which was spoken of by the prophet Joel – 'My Spirit on all flesh.'"

When the Spirit comes on our flesh it changes our world. Up until now we hadn't seen a significant move of God since the charismatic days, but thank God, he always has something more!

The early years of this decade have been dry, with hard-working men trying to achieve something for God but producing very little. We need the Holy Spirit to breathe life into our lives and churches and see our communities turned upside down with the gospel of Jesus.

In Mark 6.45 we read: "Immediately he made his disciples get into the boat and go before him to the other side, to Bethsaida, while he sent the multitude away."(NKJ)

Here we see Jesus commanding the disciples to go to the other side of the sea. All of us who serve the Lord Jesus have a sense of destiny within us: 'Go and build that church', 'Go and join that team' or 'Go and win that neighbour'. But many of us, trying figuratively to 'row our boats' and steer towards our destinations, have found the 'winds against us'.

Our evangelistic campaigns, good ideas and principles that worked elsewhere left us weary and somewhat burned out. Dry and barren, many of us were asking, 'What is the use?' But in our despair and disillusionment we found that, just as Jesus watched over them in the boat, so, too, he had seen our difficulties. Someone saw them rowing that night: working hard, with water coming into their boat and nearly down and out. And not only did he see them – and I love the next sentence – 'he made to come towards them.'

Here were men who knew Jesus really well. They had talked with him, eaten with him and lived with him, but they had never seen him like this before. Their minds could not comprehend who it was and they cried out in fear, "It's a ghost!"

Today in Sunderland he's come in a way we've never known before. It's a bit ghost-like, but he whispers in it all – in the laughter, in the shaking, in the falling down – "Be not afraid. It is I."

What did the disciples do? They invited him into their boat and the result was peace, order and calm. I thank God that we can say the same, having invited him into our boat.

Chapter 17

Breaking dividing walls

"Please forgive me," sobbed the man from Northern Ireland as he grasped the microphone from the preacher's hand.

It was Wednesday morning during our conference with Randy Clark in April 1995. As he spoke, men and women ran together to the platform weeping and embracing and repenting of hardened attitudes and judgements they had held in their hearts. We were witnessing the amazing reconciliation of brothers and sisters from Northern and Southern Ireland. Together, and in perfect unity, they prayed for their divided nation.

At this juncture, a gentleman from the south of England leapt on to the platform and repented of the attitude of superiority he felt southerners held towards those who live in the north of England. Within moments he was joined by a typically North Eastern pastor who, with tears, repented of hostility towards the south. Brother embraced brother, and two thousand people prayed and wept together with a great deal of repentance for unity in our nation.

For us, one of the major hallmarks of the move in Sunderland has been the reconciliation and unity brought about by the Holy Spirit in a unique and sovereign way. As we began to meet night after night during the month of

August 1994 God brought together an amazing amalgam of people, and our hearts were knit in a way that prior to this time would have been impossible.

For so long we have all worked within walls – 'Me in my small corner and you in yours'. It was very sobering for me as the Lord revealed my heart and showed me how my attitudes and responses to other brothers serving the Lord had been anything but glorifying to the Lord Jesus Christ. Often we can despise those who are not moving in the same flow of things as us; how proud we can be without the Spirit of God moving in our hearts. Anglican has received from the Lord alongside Baptist, Presbyterian and House church. The dividing walls are coming down.

Renewed sense of unity

The team who have helped to facilitate the renewal services have been put together by God from all streams, and we flow in a renewed sense of unity and purpose. One of these ministers had had a five-year difference with one of our own church leaders and neither had spoken to the other in all this time, so it was a joy to see them fall into each other's arms in tears and repent. Now some evenings they lead the service together.

One of the most surprising and deeply moving aspects of the last year has been the discovery of the gracious, generous and Christ-centred hearts of our Brethren brothers. Churches from Brethren roots have lent us the greatest support, and where our doctrinal and other differences separated us, we were discovering that while there were many streams we were all flowing into the same river. Jesus's prayer for the unity of the church is beginning to be fulfilled.

During the first few weeks of August 1994 two family doctors, a father and his son, began to attend the renewal services. They had come with an initial scepticism, but with hearts open to receive all that the Father had for them. Understandably, what was going on around them was far removed from anything they had experienced within their church, which had been born out of the Glanton Brethren stream.

It was difficult for them to come to Sunderland Christian Centre, since up until this point we had been seen by them as rivals and perhaps even stealers of their sheep. However, through the most amazing sacrifice and grace, Dr Leon Le Dune, presiding elder of that church, showed us an excellence of spirit that shamed us, considering our narrow, mean-spirited intolerance of the past.

After two weeks attending renewal services in our church, and to our utter amazement, Philip Le Dune, Leon's son, and I felt a knitting of our hearts. God spoke separately, to us and without doubt we knew God had drawn us together to serve him in the kingdom.

Holding up my arms

Philip began to preach in the renewal services and came very humbly one day to tell me that the Lord had clearly spoken to him calling him to the ministry, and that the Lord had called him to hold up my arms and help in the renewal. This meant that he would need to leave his home church and come and worship with us in order that he could fulfil his call. I felt it was important to speak personally with his father Leon before Philip made any decisions about his future, since without his father's blessing I would not have gone ahead.

We met one morning for coffee, and as his mother Linda sat with tears coursing down her cheeks, she and Leon affirmed that they, too, knew that God was asking them to give up their son for the purpose of the ministry. We were humbled by their spirits. They were offering to us a fine teaching gift and precious man of God; their only son. This is what renewal is all about – not empire building but kingdom building, preferring one another in love.

Leon's Story

"My whole adult life until the end of 1993 was spent in the practice of medicine, and for 24 years I was a family doctor in the same town. During that time I also served as a leader in the local church and ministered as an elder in a pastoral, teaching and preaching role.

"In the early '70s the church was powerfully affected by the Charismatic renewal, and a new era opened up for us all. However, following a time of blessing and growth, many problems arose in the life of the fellowship, so that by the late '80s and early '90s we were struggling and discouraged. I had decided to retire at the end of 1993 in order to give myself more fully to the church.

"Then one evening, about six months before the due date, I suddenly developed symptoms which I knew indicated an impending heart attack. I was admitted to hospital, and two hours after admission developed a complication which would have ended my life if I had not been in the intensive care unit. As I was returning to full consciousness I suddenly became aware of the presence of God. There was no vision or sound; simply an overwhelming sense of awesome power and tremendous love.

"In August 1994 we began to hear that some extraordinary things were happening at Sunderland Christian Centre, and that in some way this was linked with events that were taking place both in Holy Trinity, Brompton, and in Toronto, Canada. I was inclined to be dismissive and suspicious about some of the things that had been reported, but my son Philip, who was worship leader in our fellowship at that time, decided to investigate matters and went with a friend to see exactly what was happening.

"Philip told me that there were aspects of the meeting which he could not account for, but felt that God was definitely at work among his people. I then went myself, mainly to observe, but to my surprise found myself responding to the opportunity given to receive ministry. I was even more surprised to find myself flat on my back, receiving loving ministry and prayer from a brother with whom I had had a serious disagreement in the recent past. That night brought about a reconciliation in the loving purposes of God and brought me to a further crisis point in my spiritual journey.

Radically changed

"Our church has been, and continues to be, powerfully affected by this time of renewal and refreshing. We have seen, and are seeing, remarkable changes in people's lives. Problems in the lives of individuals which had proved to be virtually insurmountable have been opened up and dealt with. My own life in the Lord has been radically changed.

"As a leadership we have handed over control of our church to the Holy Spirit in a new way, which has proved to be very costly in a number of ways. Philip was released from our fellowship to serve on the team at Sunderland

Christian Centre because we recognised as a leadership that the call of God was upon his life and that in the course of God's dealings with him he had received the gift of preaching in an anointed way.

"At this stage I can only say that I am deeply grateful to the Lord for his patience with me. I feel a profound sense of privilege in being a sharer in anything that the Lord is doing at this time. There is a growing sense of excitement and anticipation among the people of God such as I have never known in my lifetime. I pray that like Caleb I may receive the grace that is available to me and all God's people to possess whatever 'mountain' he has placed before us for the taking. May the sovereign Lord lead us forward to genuine heaven-sent revival!"

Honouring one another

Forgiveness, humility and an honouring of one another is becoming the hallmark of those at the forefront of the move.

Randy Clark, during a visit to Sunderland in the early summer of 1995, said that he had for a long time had a major problem with the so called 'faith camp' led by Kenneth Copeland and others – he had sternly preached against it. However, God had rebuked him for his 'mean-spiritedness', and on a visit to Kenneth Hagin's Rhema Bible Church he was moved when he saw how the people had given up so much for Jesus, and he asked the leadership to forgive him. "I honour you because you love Jesus," he told them publicly, at which point a Baptist minister asked Randy's forgiveness for having written an article against him.

Amusingly I, too, did a great deal of repenting when it

was to a Vineyard church I had to go to receive of the Holy Spirit. Prior to this I had actively discouraged anyone attending conferences where John Wimber was speaking, and refused to listen to any worship tapes. Vineyard was not to my taste, but God has dealt with me, too!

So it is that the renewal in Sunderland could not have been maintained without the selfless support of many other churches from all over the North-East of all denominations. Truly we have been living under commanded blessing, because of such unity.

The scriptures tell us in Psalm 133: "Behold, how good and how pleasant it is for brethren to dwell together in unity! It is like the precious oil upon the head, running down on the beard, the beard of Aaron, running down on the edge of his garments. It is like the dew of Hermon descending upon the mountains of Zion; for there the Lord commanded the blessing – life forevermore."(NKJ)

It is a great thing to be under the blessing of God, but it is even better to know that you are experiencing 'commanded blessing'.

Spotless bride

In Genesis 1 we read the story of creation. This account of creation in Genesis 1:2 gives us a picture of what the church can look like from time to time: "Without form, void and darkness on the face of the deep." I believe the Holy Spirit has been hovering for years over the church, waiting for the command to go forth to bring to it shape and substance, and to bring into fulfilment the pure, spotless bride the Son so passionately seeks.

The problem for so many of us has been that because the body of Christ has been so fractured, the Father has been unable to issue a command of blessing and so the Holy Spirit has been powerless to move. In the Genesis account of creation there was complete and perfect unity between the Father, Son and Holy Spirit. Nothing hindered; anything was possible. Jesus's prayer in John 17 is that we should be one, but every time we resist reconciliation and persist in harbouring resentment and petty jealousies we are tying the hands of God.

Things that unite

We have been aware in these days that God is able to give us so much more than we have ever known before. However, because of the drawing and wooing of his Spirit, we are much more ready to cross the denominational barriers and find those things that unite rather than those things that have divided us for years. We sit in church with born-again and spirit-filled Christians of all traditions and feel that we are one body.

I'm sure, however, that God wants this to become much more than the ability to sit in church together. He wants us to actively work together in building the kingdom, to be a support to one another and to protect each other.

This is a taste of the Acts of the Apostles, when the togetherness of the early disciples caused God to lavish such joy and power that they overcame all external opposition. In the days ahead, there is no doubt in my mind that it is this calibre of mutual Christian commitment that will restore integrity to the church and see God's authority much more clearly demonstrated in the world.

Chapter 18

The Garden of God

Since August 1994 we in Sunderland, along with churches all over the world, have been seeing hearts restored to the Father. The prodigals are returning, the orphan spirit is being replaced by the spirit of adoption and we are crying "Abba Father" from hearts that have been touched by the love of God. Thousands upon thousands of people are testifying to the fact that they have returned to their first love with an increased intimacy and passion. What we seem to be understanding a little more is that God is trying to get us to love him from the heart, not just understand Him with our heads.

In Genesis 2:15 we read that God took man and put him in the Garden of Eden to tend and keep it. He had the responsibility to cultivate the garden, not only for himself but also as a place where God could take pleasure in those that he loved with an everlasting love. God loves our fellowship, and he longs to pour his love, his passionate love, upon us. Time and time again the scriptures show us a Father intimately involved in the life of his children. In particular, the story of the prodigal son clearly describes to us a seeing, running, hugging, kissing, party-throwing Father!

The Song of Solomon describes 'the beloved', comparing his bride to 'a garden, enclosed, a spring shut up, a fountain sealed'. This garden enclosed, sealed and private was reserved only for the King. His garden was a unique place of pleasure and rest, and he went there simply to be refreshed by its beauty. The bride never allowed her gates to be left standing open in order to protect the garden from animals and strangers wandering in. The heart of the bride should not be open to the polluting spirit of this world; her garden needs to be locked and sealed, kept only for her 'beloved'.

A walled garden

In Genesis we see God putting Adam in the garden to tend and keep it, while today we see the Holy Spirit tending and keeping the garden of our hearts. As he does so we need always to maintain a sealed, walled garden, closed to immorality, pride and greed.

Therefore, it is not surprising that the majority of testimonies during this move of God bear witness to the fact that the Father is dealing with the issues of the heart. Weeds and thorns are being lifted by the roots, and the King is taking pleasure in his garden.

For most of us, as we have done 'carpet time'[1], hearts have been laid bare and areas that have long since been closed off are being turned over to the Father.

Our own Lil McGill, one of the original 'Dales Six', during ministry time one evening was suddenly reminded of an incident thirteen years before when, after major surgery a doctor broke the news that she would be unable to have any more children. All her grief, anger and frustration was directed at the one bearing the bad news, and she felt great resentment towards the medical profession. As the Holy Spirit began to move, the Lord gently revealed to her that since that time part of her heart had been closed off to him as bitterness and resentment took root. She repented, and opened up her heart, and now the King is taking pleasure in his garden.

Another lady in our church asked the Lord to come and change her heart, when he responded by telling her he was unable to do so. In astonishment she asked him why. Immediately she had a vision of her own heart, and across it was a large chain with a sign saying 'No Entry'. With repentance and tears she took down the sign and God came and tended to her heart.

Deep inner healings are being accomplished in an incredibly short time. Outward manifestations often are a pointer to the work deep in an individual heart. Though by no means do we decry counselling, we have discovered that in ten minutes on the carpet, God accomplished what years of counselling have been unable to do.

Children were profoundly touched

The children were the first to be deeply and profoundly touched when God broke out in our church last August.

One of our staff prior to her conversion had suffered a particularly difficult bereavement; her husband was killed in confusing and difficult circumstances.

As her life fell apart, she turned increasingly to the solace of alcohol. Understandably, her children were aware of the drama being played out around them.

After her dramatic conversion, she grew spiritually in leaps and bounds, but had a growing problem with her eldest daughter, who was terrified to leave her mother and cried inconsolably when forced to go to school. Frequently the headmistress of the junior school had no alternative but to send the child home.

When the time came for transfer to senior school, the situation had become impossible. Tutors and the Head of House kindly but firmly suggested that the Educational Psychological Services were the only answer.

How wonderful God is, he provided his divine answer in the week after our return from Toronto. This child was one of the first to lay peacefully on the carpet receiving from the hand of the Lord.

I am always with you

When she went home, she realised to her dismay she had a slight 'jerk' and immediately wondered how she could explain it to her friends. However, that evening she felt the Lord had said to her: "You only jerk because from time to time I give you a little touch from my hand, to remind you that I am always with you, you are never alone." Immediately her fear of separation from her mother was over. School in September was no longer a problem, her confidence grew and she matured in leaps and bounds.

Three months later the school tutor wrote to her parents: "Natalie has grown in confidence at an almost unbelievable rate. She now relates well to her peers and is improving all the time in her contact with adults." Her Head of House reported: "Dear Mrs Wilson, I am so very impressed with Natalie's attitude to school – what a change. No longer do we need the help of the Educational Psychological Services as Natalie has increased dramatically in confidence."

Frank's story

For some years Frank Hutchins had been totally miserable, making his own, his family's and everyone else's life a misery. After a successful managerial career he was made redundant and found it impossible to find another job. He felt his usefulness was over, life had condemned him to the scrap heap.

As his self-esteem plunged even lower, Frank was convinced his family would reject him, and he endeavoured to make himself so unappealing that he would help them along the way. He rejected them before they could inflict pain on him. Grace, his wife, had reached the end of the road and, having visited Sunderland Christian Centre and been ministered to at the point of her deepest need, she persuaded Frank to come along. Angry, isolated and confused, he sat apart, an observer, not a participator.

Finally his son, home from the Royal Navy, asked Herbert to pray for his father. Frank crawled home that evening!

He and Grace have lived in happy harmony ever since, he feels he has been born anew and we all love him! In fact, Frank has been an invaluable help in our office: if you have attended a conference in Sunderland he was probably the one who processed your registration. He is a changed man.

Reconciliation

One of the most moving testimonies of the renewal has been a story of reconciliation. One lady, after years of living in angry, bitter solitude, having been divorced acrimoniously years ago, turned up at a renewal service. She had travelled some distance to be there. Her husband, not knowing she was present, also turned up at the service. After the Holy Spirit had touched her heart during the ministry time, Millie felt she should ask her ex-husband if he could ever forgive her. Unknown to her, God was also dealing with his heart and he felt prompted to ask if she could ever love him again. The upshot of this story is that they were re-married this summer!

God is doing amazing things, and we give him all the glory.

---

[1] 'Doing carpet time' – a newly coined phrase meaning resting in the spirit.

Chapter 19

Ministers Refreshed

Sunderland was now proving to be an oasis for church leaders who had become spiritually dry and barren. Many pastors who were ready to give up the ministry were profoundly changed, re-empowered and re-envisioned.

In October 1994, whilst in Toronto for the 'Catch the Fire' conference, I was asked to testify as to what God was doing in Sunderland, but I was so powerfully moved by the presence of God that all I could say was, "The church is coming together." Mark Dupont, a prophet from Toronto who has a powerful world-wide ministry, and interestingly who prophesied the events to come in the Airport Vineyard Church, began to speak over Lois and myself: "You have a vision for the nations," he said. "I see a vision of a large star over the two of you. Just as the star of Bethlehem brought wise men to the baby Jesus, so the Lord will bring wise men in the body of Christ to you. In your weakness and child-like simplicity God will bring many leaders to you. Yours is the ministry of the baby Jesus, and the Lord is going to open up doors and bring political leaders to you."

Since then we have seen denominational leaders come all the way across the globe specifically to receive from

God in Sunderland. Many pastors and church leaders have come from Australia, whilst others have flown from Africa, Europe, Asia and the United States. Not only have they themselves been profoundly affected but, by taking the blessing back, they have also been keys in spreading it to other parts of the world in their travels.

A 'down-under' experience

David Cartledge, the church planting co-ordinator for the AOG in Australia, had a 'down-under' experience when he came to Sunderland. "My wife and I spent much of the meeting on the floor under the power of God," he said later. "Lois asked me to come and share a testimony immediately after the worship time, but I was struck dumb – unable to speak at all – and spent the next hour-and-a-half on the floor being mightily touched by God's power. My whole body was being jolted as though electrodes were being put against my chest."

Whilst in Brisbane shortly before his visit, David had experienced a powerful new encounter with God after a friend returned from a world trip a changed man following an experience with God in Sunderland.

"When I saw the passion for Jesus that had erupted in his life it began to show my relationship with the Lord in stark relief," David recalled. "It left me feeling somewhat empty; that my life was on the simmer, not on the boil. I became terribly depressed and didn't know what to do, but I cried out for more of God. The following weekend I was speaking in Brisbane and after a good response to the altar call I felt the Lord say, 'Don't lay hands on anybody.' And before I could leave the platform people were falling to the floor."

Then, as he was praying for someone, David amazingly froze like a statue for a full 15 minutes.

"I wondered what had gone wrong and was scared to death," he said. "Then God spoke to me, saying: 'I just wanted you to see what I can do if I can get you out of the way.' And that was the beginning of a spiritual revolution that was to turn my life upside down."

David now says he is seeing more people come to Christ than ever before and has also seen revival sweep through the Southern Cross Bible College, of which he is president.

He tells of how a group of students on a staircase discussing all that God was doing were suddenly visited as on the Day of Pentecost, and all six were slain in the spirit with laughing, crying, shaking and trembling. As other students ran out to see what was happening the power of God hit them, too, so that over forty students were laid out on the floor, some of them for over five hours. Describing the turn-around in his own life, David says, "I have experienced an incredible change in myself – an intensified love for Jesus and his word and a passion for souls that has come out of a refreshing of the Holy Spirit in my life. The Spirit has come with power in a way that I have not previously experienced.

"This new move is having a great impact on Australia. A number of our ministers have been mightily touched of God in Sunderland, and although many of our pastors including myself, have been to Toronto – and it has been a blessing – I believe there is much more in the world through the work of the Spirit than what is happening in Toronto. I do believe we are in the beginning of a mighty worldwide revival, and I am committed to being in the very centre of the river of the Spirit of God."

Andrew Evans, superintendent of the AOG in Australia, has also preached during this time of renewal in our church in Sunderland. He challenged us not to take for granted the wonderful open heaven we were living under at this time.

Renewed passion

Pastors from Europe have regularly joined with us in praying for our continent, and it has been our privilege to pray with them that they may return to their countries with a fire in their hearts and a renewed passion for their Saviour.

A pastor from Helsinki, Rauno Kokkola, of the Greater Helsinki Church, visited Sunderland in early spring. He and his wife had decided if God did not move in their church by Easter of 1995 then they were returning to the USA.

Rauno says his faith grew to believe that that which was happening in Sunderland could begin in Helsinki. At the Easter services God broke in sovereignly, and now they are running nightly services and reaching many from the former Soviet Union and the whole of Scandinavia.

For the past six months we as a church have set up a scheme called 'Aid to the Nations', whereby we regularly give finance to bring Eastern European pastors and leaders over to conferences. During our conference with Randy Clark at the end of May 1995, it was our privilege to bring over six Albanian pastors, who were powerfully impacted. One of them, an Anglican priest, has since written apologising for all his critical judgements prior to his visit. During one service, quite spontaneously, laughter came upon him and he laughed and laughed until the tears streamed down his face. Within one week of his return to Albania, our office received a telephone call from him excitedly reporting thirty-five decisions for Christ in his first Sunday evening service after returning home!

An AOG pastor, David Parry, of the North Road Christian Fellowship in Preston, Lancashire, was desperately discouraged in the summer of 1994 – his many evangelistic enterprises had reaped pitiful results, and he had also come under personal attack and had seen several people leave the church.

He felt spiritually drained and completely isolated, and recorded in his devotional diary: "I have nothing to give; I cannot continue with this farce; I must get away from the round of ministry. Does that crushing emptiness come from God, to excavate the hole of my need so that he can fill it..?"

Having told other members of his leadership group that he could not minister again until he had met with God and received something new, he left for Sunderland on Thursday September 13th to spend a few days at the renewal. That few days turned into a week!

A huge smile on the inside

Having overcome his initial need to rationalise and understand what he saw going on around him there, he began to let God take control. On the second night, as he lay on the carpet, God's power hit him with fresh force. The following night, he remembers, it was as if the Lord had painted a huge smile on his inside. Writing in his diary he said: "All the pain of the past months, the frustration, hurt and emptiness was replaced by that internal smile." For him

Psalm 23 came alive as he felt God causing him to lie down in green pastures 'to restore his soul'. By the time Sunday evening came, his smile on the inside had broken out into waves of laughter, but the best was yet to come.

On the final evening of his visit, Philip Le Dune, the family doctor spoken of earlier, was preaching on King David, the man after God's own heart. Using his experience as a doctor, he reminded us that had he been a plumber he would have spoken to us about pipes and water, and had he been a mechanic he may have spoken about engines and oil. But as a family doctor the Holy Spirit prompted him to talk about blindness. He explained that if one eye was weak, the medical prescription for such a lazy eye would be a patch over the good eye. This, he said, would force the weaker eye to work much harder and thus strengthen the muscles. Perhaps, he suggested, God was covering the well developed eye of our understanding so as to strengthen the weaker eye of the heart.

Revolutionised

Suddenly David knew within himself that God wanted him to get up and shout "I want a heart like that." He battled against doing such an outrageous thing, especially as a pastor in a public meeting, but finally – under such a strong anointing that he was unable to stand – he crawled out to the front. Taking the microphone from the preacher's hand, he spoke the words before breaking down in tears in front of the hundreds of people present that night. His life and ministry were revolutionised, and the fire of the Lord fell on his return to Preston. An awesome presence of God came upon the church, accompanied by many powerful manifestations and the fruit of changed lives.

Malcolm Thomas, pastor of the AOG church in Morpeth, came to the renewal meetings in August 1994 purely out of commitment to us as a friend. He was very sceptical, and as the service progressed he was appalled when he realised that we were worshipping along to accompanying tapes, since many of the renewal songs were unknown to us and our musicians – we simply had not had time to learn them.

Early on in the service God began to move powerfully, and when Lois cried out 'God wants his church back' Malcolm was knocked back two or three rows, carrying Herbert Harrison along with him. Since then he has lovingly told us how he said to God: "If you are going to be that violent, then you can have your church back!" Malcolm has never been the same since and is one of the team of ministers who preaches weekly in the services, and about thirty of his people regularly serve in the renewal meetings.

Cyril Collins a very down-to-earth pastor with a theology degree would only drop his wife off at the door and then pick her up again afterwards. After much persuasion he attended the church on the same night that Malcolm Thomas was touched, heard his daughter share how she had been wonderfully changed and then as the cry rang out 'God wants his church back', he, too, was violently thrown across the chairs and into the aisle. Now he knew it was God, and he has been one of the most valuable members of the renewal team since that night.

Changed hearts

Another pastor whose heart has been profoundly changed during the renewal has been British evangelist David Nellist, who had seen many amazing signs and wonders over 28 years of successful ministry around the world. He was recovering from a breakdown when God led him to pioneer a work in Scarborough. He had heard all about what was happening in Sunderland, and his first visit was in the Autumn of 1994 at one of the monthly leaders' meetings.

David remembers that as he walked through the doors he was aware of the very real presence of God. He didn't go forward for prayer, but just remained seated and drank it in. He didn't want to move, since it was wonderful to feel the presence of the Lord like that again. Later he confessed that he had become a professional preacher, only spending time with God when he needed a new sermon to preach. God changed his heart and now he has a passion for Jesus.

The outworking of that passion came in the breaking down of yet another dividing wall. Gerald Coates, leader of the Pioneer Group of Churches, was speaking at a leaders' day early in 1995. David had actually preached against him from the pulpit. In his own words, he thought that: "Gerald was the most horrendous heretic around. I felt very bitter towards him, and I would never have crossed doors to hear him, never mind drive all the way from Scarborough – a distance of about 85 miles!"

I would have to apologise

"I realised how much God had done in my heart. I had been very judgmental before and fought back tears all the way to the meeting because I knew I was going to have to apologise for my attitude. God was dealing with me about it. During the afternoon session I went forward and Gerald prophesied over me – you would have thought he knew everything about my life. I tell you I really sobbed. It was just like God. He used the very man I used to criticise to really speak into my life. I stayed until the very end of the evening meeting, after midnight, to see him and apologised for the things I had said about him in the past. He showed me such grace as he thanked me and put his arms around me. God has really turned me inside out; I was wearing a mask for years and now I am back in the river of God."

A big change of heart

Closer to home, local pastors were also being powerfully affected. Among them was Mark Drew, minister of the Elim Pentecostal Church in Sunderland. His problem with Sunderland Christian Centre had nothing to do with doctrine; he was simply jealous of our success, and has publicly confessed that he used to drive around the premises and gloat when he saw that the vandals had smashed our windows. But he had a big change of heart.

Mark was on the point of resigning – he had already written the letter after the hardest six months of his twenty-five year ministry – when the Spirit of God broke into his life. Today he is rejuvenated and renewed in his call.

The Assemblies of God magazine 'Joy' has devoted much space to this refreshing. Following a remarkable move of the Holy Spirit in the Tuesday morning business session of the denomination's general conference, the organisers arranged an unscheduled 'Times of Refreshing' meeting, and the main ballroom was filled with people seeking more of God.

Peter Wreford, editor of the magazine, was so moved by the Spirit that he was virtually struck dumb when asked by Lois to testify. All he could say in the end was "Please pray for me", after which he was immersed once more in the river of blessing.

Later he wrote: "Fuelled by visits to the renewal meetings in Sunderland, I arrived at Sonrise in a state of spiritual barrenness and acutely aware of my own weakness, yet with the expectation that God must surely move.

"My fervent desire not to miss out in the time of God's blessing was tempered by a resolve not to make it up. It had to be the real thing! I was determined I would not fall down unless the Holy Spirit did it. I would not 'manifest' to please those praying for me.

"Deadlines prevented me arriving before Tuesday, but exciting accounts immediately confirmed that the Holy Spirit was at work. For me the next three days proved to be a time of unimaginable blessing.

Abandonment to the Holy Spirit

"Outstanding preaching was eclipsed time and again as the congregations surged forward to receive prayer with dramatic results. Personally I began to experience the anointing of the Holy Spirit in a more powerful measure than I had ever known, resulting in a physical longing for God, an abandonment to the Holy Spirit and an almost complete lack of awareness of those around me.

"I did not reach the point where I felt I must beg the Lord to send no more, but I did feel that point was close. Subsequent feelings extremely similar to the effects of alcohol strongly affected me as I tried to walk and avoid laughing at everything.

"Though I'm normally very reserved, the Holy Spirit had turned me into a shouting, jerking drunk - but boy, am I glad!

"The next morning an unscheduled renewal meeting with Ken and Lois gave opportunity for still more. Called to the platform by Lois, I found myself unable to speak. Able only to ask for prayer, I experienced extreme movings of the Holy Spirit and resorted to sitting on the edge of the stage – still determined not to fall, even though I was incapable of standing up.

"In prayer, as the meeting progressed, I finally felt that I was in danger of being obstructive to the Holy Spirit and decided I would no longer determinedly resist falling. Raising my hands in prayer with my eyes tightly shut, my fingers brushed Lois' hand as she happened to be standing nearby. And as I did so a seemingly explosive force sent me crashing from my sitting position to the floor. At all times I felt I might be able to control myself, but any desire to get up had now left me and I simply enjoyed basking in the love of God and receiving faith and revelations beyond my imagination."

Since the renewal hit it has not just been young men and women who have been envisioned and empowered for service. Some of the more elderly, if I dare say that, have had equally life-changing experiences. At 73 my father-in-law, Herbert Harrison, is one such person and, in his own words, he recounts his experience:

Herbert Harrison's story

"When the so-called 'Toronto blessing' first hit our local church in Sunderland, my attitude was, at first, one of cautious approval. 'Test the spirits' and 'Prove all things' were scriptures I had applied to many disputable innovations over a long pastorate in Newcastle-upon-Tyne.

"My stand was much like Gamaliel's in Acts chapter 5:

If this is God it will bear good fruit, if it isn't it will peter out as just another fad, so leave it alone and see what happens. Actually, cautious fence-sitters like Gamaliel will never move mountains; it is the risk-takers like Caleb who, even in old age, refused to be intimidated by the giants of apathy and opposition, who take mountains.

"So it was that I had made up my mind not to be reactionary in my judgement of the physical manifestations. If the devil pushed some to extremes and the truth is hurt in the process I would try not to react negatively and 'throw out the baby with the bath water.' The devil is a past master at getting folk to close their minds to things they don't fully understand.

"I felt uncomfortable at first with the variety of manifestations, but as R T Kendall, of Westminster Chapel, said: 'I would rather handle electricity with wet hands than say that what is happening is of the devil.' From time to time over the last year I have been asked if any of the physical manifestations have happened to me and I have to answer, honestly, 'No' – even though I am open as far as I know how to be. I have no compelling need to receive any external evidence of God's acceptance of me because my focus is not on what happens on the outside but on Jesus Christ and what he wants to do in me and through me.'

Love strengthened

"My love for him has been strengthened as I have prayed with literally hundreds from all over the UK and many other parts of the world and have witnessed the coming of the Holy Spirit upon them in powerful ways - many have been instantly healed and delivered from phobias, while others have been converted to Christ on the spot.

"I should add that it has been my privilege to assist many to positive experiences in God who have found it difficult to receive because of little or no physical reaction to the prayer of faith. A physical manifestation is not the only evidence of a life touched by the Spirit. Jesus said: 'Blessed are those who have not seen, yet believe.'

"Like Caleb of old, I see the challenge of Britain without God as a mountain to take. I fully accept that God is sovereignly refreshing, equipping and empowering his church: 'But you shall receive power when the Holy Spirit has come upon you; and you shall be my witnesses in Jerusalem, and in all Judea and Samaria, and to the ends of the earth.'(Acts 1:8).

City-shaking

"I see all that is happening as a renewing work of grace that must break out into an Acts of the Apostles-type of city-shaking, society-changing experience if it is to avoid becoming a protracted, self-interested brand of ministry unworthy of God.

"With the glorious prospect in mind of thousands coming to Christ on the wave of what is possibly the last great move of the Spirit before Jesus returns, the Sunderland church have decided to send Mary and I to Argentina following a powerful conference with Ed Silvoso. Fresh from the revival where literally millions of Argentinians have come to Christ in the last 12 years, he encouraged us to have faith for God to do it here. My heart is excited when I contemplate the current trickle of converts becoming a veritable river of humanity coming to find life and fulfilment in Jesus. I am full of anticipation for the next wave of revival, ushering in the lost multitudes. Let it come Lord!

"I believe that just as Sunderland Christian Centre has become a model for renewal, so it is God's intention that it should become a model for taking cities for God. By word of mouth, the blessing of God in Sunderland has touched all five continents, and by word of mouth the more localised Sunderland community will be reached because God is able to do it.

"Powerful prophetic voices have brought strong directives touching the expansion of the vision to reach the lost. It is for us to pray that vision into being, just as Elijah did after God had given him revelation that rain showers were coming; he prayed and prayed again until he saw the cloud as big as a man's hand coming over the sea.

"So we must not see renewal as an end in itself, but pray the purpose of God into being, keeping alive the vision for our communities."

Chapter 20

Where do we go from here?

A group of Brazilian pastors visiting Britain recently said that a cloud of revival is already on the horizon of our nation. They had come from a revival situation and when asked at the 'Pray for Revival' conference what they had from God for this country they declared: "There is a cloud on the horizon, as in the Elijah story, and it can only get bigger. There are wells of pure water in this country. We drank of those wells, but you must go on clearing them. The water is pure, but they are clogged up with things like theology, wrong traditions and lack of faith. We can see things happening in Britain that began to happen in Brazil as the revival there started."

Revelation 22:1: "And he showed me a pure river of the water of life, clear as crystal, proceeding from the throne of God."(NKJ)

The river that leaves the throne room is as clear as crystal and in this present move of the Spirit, God is inviting us to drink from his river which flows straight from his throne room! Often we have been drinking from contaminated, polluted water full of our own ideas and selfish ambitions, but now the invitation has come to move upstream where the water is clearer and unpolluted.

153

Recently John Glass, the senior pastor of the Church of God in Kilsyth, Scotland, preached in one of our renewal services on this very subject.

He had been to Spain and whilst reflecting on the plane flying over there he wondered whether or not he should be going as he had 101 other things he could be doing. Meeting the pastor on his arrival seemed to reinforce this argument; he was an elderly gentleman who had recently had major heart surgery, and his pacemaker could be visibly seen as it pulsed away in his chest. This was not your stereotype for charismatic leadership.

The presence of the Lord

However, when John arrived at the church, full of doubts as to what he might encounter, he was amazed to find an incredible sense of the presence of the Lord in the place.

And this was not a one-off experience; it happened night after night after night.

He was curious as to why this should be and before leaving asked the pastor to explain the reason for such obvious spiritual intensity in his church. The answer amazed him; it was not what he would normally expect to hear. Looking at his departing guest the pastor simply said: "Not one person in my church has a television."

Surely this could not be right; it had to be something deeper or more profound than that. Interestingly God had already spoken to John on the subject just a few months before. As he relaxed with his wife one evening watching a major soap on the television, he suddenly realised that the story line was centred around a public house, a betting shop or a house in which the unmarried couple were living together.

He decided to go on a television fast for a month and the results were staggering. During his own church meetings there was an increased awareness of the presence of God, and a member who had suffered from excruciating pain in his knees for 18 years and was even considering a private operation costing many thousands of pounds, was spontaneously and miraculously healed by the power of God – free from pain at last. Others also testified to being healed and having their spiritual passion renewed.

It wasn't a sense of legalistic duty that set John on his fast, but a deep desire God had put in his heart to drink from a clearer stream. He believes that by starving his mind of contamination from the television screen he simply moved further upstream, nearer to the throne room where the water was pure.

Let us be willing to do the same.

An open heaven

Argentinian evangelist Ed Silvoso, fresh from the revival situation in Argentina, on a recent visit to Sunderland prophesied forthcoming revival, and Andrew Evans, general superintendent of the AOG in Australia visiting Sunderland in April 1995, encouraged us by saying that he felt we were living under an open heaven, which he compared to Seoul, Korea, where Yonggi Cho has a church congregation equivalent in size to the population of Leeds, a major city in West Yorkshire.

This open heaven, I am sure, is a direct result of protracted services, with prayer, worship and praise being lifted to God every evening.

We must believe that the move of the Spirit in our

nation, which is now reported to have touched over 5,000 churches, will affect the social structure and national conscience of this land.

After the Lord turned over the tables of the money changers in the temple, he then proclaimed that his house would be called 'a house of prayer'. In a very real sense the Holy Spirit has come and turned over the tables of some of our practices, and now I am convinced that passionate and persistent prayer for revival, as has been the model in Korea and Argentina, is part of the next phase of the current move of God.

This is not the end

At our celebration of one year of meeting every evening, Wes Richards prophesied that "this is not the end but is the beginning of a great move of God. There will come a powerful increase of angelic visitation and awareness of heaven. There will be a far-reaching world dimension, and the network of unity in this area will be pulled in more tightly."

However much we all want to spread the fire throughout the world, we must remember that passion and zeal can never be an excuse for disobeying the word of God. History has shown us that mistakes can be made – especially during an outpouring of the mercy and grace of God.

We need to ensure that rather than having less of the Word, we have a greater passion for the scriptures. We don't need less prayer, but more effective prayer; nor less fellowship, but greater commitment and love within the body. An abundance of grace can never give us licence to ignore the guidelines laid down for us in scripture. We still need their protection.

King David decided to ignore the instructions given by God for the transportation of the ark, and rather than have it carried on the shoulders of the priests, he placed it on a new cart. The Philistines transported the ark in this way, and a valuable lesson can be learned here. The ways and methods of the world can never be those of the church; they are unable to carry the presence of God. We need anointed leadership to carry this move of God to its final destination. It might take a little longer and it may not look as slick and polished this way, but it's the way God wants it.

With all that we are involved in, there are times when we come to difficult periods and, for David, Nachon's threshing floor was such a place. Uzzah – meaning strength – reached out to steady the ark as it became unstable on the rough ground of the threshing floor. Too often the arm of the flesh is put out to steady what is perceived to be unstable.

Uzzah was struck dead and David feared God so much that he wouldn't touch the ark or move any further with it. The king didn't want to touch it; the priests didn't want to touch it, but a little insignificant 'nobody' called Obed-Edom stepped forward. He was willing to take the ark, even though others were afraid.

Blessing beyond measure

The scripture tells us that God blessed Obed-Edom and all his household. Why? Because he accommodated the presence of God. And if we are prepared to stretch and enlarge, push back the limits and broaden to accommodate God in all his fullness, we, too, will know his blessing in our lives beyond measure.

Many insignificant and unknown Obed-Edoms are

coming forward today, and despite many things which could deter them, they are saying: "I'll take the ark."

As God has brought leaders of all denominations together in Sunderland to serve in the renewal, we have been challenged to regularly meet for prayer for the region. We are encouraged by the fact that unity at this level in Argentina has sparked major revival. As many as 280 individual homes have also been designated as homes enlisted to pray for the streets and communities surrounding them.

One of the church staff and her family began to pray for their neighbours who were having a time of great trouble. Weeks later the lady of the family knocked on their door to thank them for praying. Astonished, they asked her how she knew this is what they had been doing. Looking slightly embarrassed, she asked them not to think her weird but she had felt their prayers coming through the wall! The outcome of all this was that she, her sister and friend have found the Lord Jesus Christ as their own personal Saviour and are now fully integrated into our church family.

Glorious individuality

Toronto Airport Vineyard have a unique task and calling to cause fire to be ignited in hearts and spread throughout the world. That fire once received is imbibed into the genetics of our own churches. In simple terms, all of us in our individual situations, having received the blessing, work out the fruit with a unique flavour of our own. As all the different streams and denominations have come together, we have not lost the glorious individuality of the local church.

As a local church, Sunderland Christian Centre has had the most remarkable year of our history.

Only months prior to this move of God, the Lord clearly spoke to me after reading Colin Dye's book, 'Building a City Church'[1], of the need to move into the area of church planting. Amazingly we have also been able to plant two churches this year.

Our initial plant in South Shields came about in a most remarkable way as a direct result of the winds of the Spirit blowing upon our hearts. Two churches laid down their leadership, one church gave up their building and our own group from Sunderland joined together in unity to form the basis of the new church, comprising 112 adults plus children. Only the unity prevalent at this time could have made this possible! Remarkably, the same thing has also happened in Washington, Tyne and Wear. This truly is God at work.

The most exciting vision

However, the most exciting vision God has given us for the coming days is stretching us as a church family once again in terms of faith, finance and sacrifice, exactly as he did in the early days of our church.

One evening six months ago during, a renewal service, a fierce-looking, well-built young man stood at the back of the hall and watched intently throughout the service. I learned later that he was the man who ran the prostitution and illegal drugs in the area, and worked for the criminal underworld carrying out violent acts at their instruction. His girlfriend had regularly been attending the renewal, and disturbed by this, and seeing all the cars at our service, Jim came to see if anybody was making money.

It was his intention to come and 'sort me out'; in other words impose his will upon mine! Thanks be to God for his wonderful protection, as he made his way determinedly to the front of the church the Holy Spirit 'punched' him before he could punch me and he fell in a heap at the foot of the platform! Sometime later, as he got up off the floor with tears streaming down his cheeks, one of our elders had the privilege of leading him to Christ.

Within months Jim had married his live-in girlfriend and now he is passionate for souls and is winning the underworld to Jesus Christ! We are unable to disclose in print just how much the Father is doing except to ask that those who read this book pray for the men of crime who are turning to Jesus and need his protection over their lives, since naturally-speaking they are now at risk after renouncing their former lives. My father-in-law, Herbert, now has a very interesting nurture group!

Vibrant with the love of Jesus

These men have a hunger to see their own community vibrant with the love of Jesus – the very community where our own church is built. They passionately want to see the young men of violence and crime, turn to the Lord and avoid the life of prison sentences that they themselves have experienced.

Whilst visiting us, Ed Silvoso prophetically saw the security fence being taken down, and I cheered in my spirit when I heard those words, as they confirmed the vision God had planted in my heart.

Our own church is now too small to hold our congregation. Thanks to all that has gone on in the last three years we have outgrown that which we gave so sacrificially to construct. As we move to a larger place, most likely a warehouse building more easily accessible and with adequate parking, it would seem sensible to sell up and off-load our building which, as I said earlier, carries a considerable mortgage. But God has told us otherwise.

As these 'Nicky Cruz'[2]-type men come to the Lord, we now have an access to the local community, and our third church plant will take place there. Part of the building will be recreational, open to the young men menacing the streets at this present time. The whole structure of our city is about to change as these men turn it around for the Lord!

If we lose the passion for souls, we have lost everything. When we are not reaching out for the lost, we cease being a church.

So we as a church will stretch ourselves again to finance a mission to those dear to the heart of the Lord: 'The Rock' church is about to be birthed and we begin again to stretch in faith and finance, and sacrifice as we did once before.

We thank God from the overflow of hearts full of love for him. We give him all the glory.

[1] 'Building a City Church' by Colin Dye – published by Kingsway.

[2] Nicky Cruz is the young gang member who was saved, as reported in the book 'The Cross and the Switchblade' (by David Wilkerson – published by Marshall Pickering) and later wrote his own story in 'Run Baby Run' – published by Hodder & Stoughton.

Appendix A

What is going on?

Strangely enough the early Pentecostals always placed a lot of emphasis on manifestations.

The question is: Are they helpful? We know, both from scripture and experience, that speaking in tongues has great benefits, making us bolder, stronger Christians. So what of shaking, laughing, falling, groaning and the many other phenomena we are seeing now?

A time to laugh!

Laughter is among the most controversial aspects of the renewal. Yet the Bible tells us that laughter is medicine for the soul and that the joy of the Lord is our strength, a fact now borne out by medical science. And it has occurred on previous occasions when God has moved powerfully on his people.

Many, including myself, have talked of 'uncontrollable laughter', when perhaps what we really mean is that we are carried away by it – not that it is totally out of control. When it first happened to me I knew I could have stopped what was happening but I didn't want to. It seemed that it was easier to continue. And I hadn't enjoyed myself like that for ages anyway.

But even as far back as the time of Abraham we read how Sarah responded to the birth of Isaac: "God has brought me laughter, and everyone who hears about this will laugh with me."(Genesis 21:6) The birth of Isaac was the physical manifestation of the supernatural intervention of God and it brought laughter. Like Isaac, we are children of promise, and in fulfilment of God's promise to pour out his Spirit on all flesh in the last days, we are filled with laughter. Isaiah says 'joy and gladness' will come to those who seek the Lord and that when we thirst after the living God 'we will go out in joy'.

The angels announced the birth of the Saviour as 'good news of great joy', much of which is manifested physically – prisoners are freed, the lame walk and the blind see. The gospel offers the 'oil of gladness instead of mourning, and a garment of praise instead of a spirit of despair.'(Isaiah 61:3) And since Britain's surgeries are crowded with patients suffering from depression, we could all do with a healthy dose of holy laughter! Ecclesiastes says there is 'a time to laugh', while the Apostle Peter describes faith in Christ as 'joy inexpressible'. And Jesus, referring to those who acknowledge their spiritual poverty, said: 'Blessed are those who weep now, for they shall laugh.'(Luke 6:21) Speaking of the Holy Spirit and the need for fellowship and obedience, he said: 'I have told you this so that my joy may be in you and that your joy may be full.'(John 15:11) Jesus wants us to be filled with his joy!

Falling at his feet!

Meanwhile, many churches and Bible Weeks look more like battlefields these days with folk falling down all over the place. Though nothing new in Pentecostal and charismatic circles, the phenomenon is now much more widespread – a fact no doubt related to a more powerful presence of God in our midst. Australian church leader David Cartledge says it's a wonder anyone is able to stand up – you may remember he spent all evening on the floor at SCC after being struck dumb as he began to testify.

In fact, every revival had traces of the manifestations we are seeing now. The Salvationists used to stack those who fell prostrate on racks...decently and in order! Smith Wigglesworth saw such scenes when he attended Salvationist meetings as a teenager in the 1870's. In his book 'The Wigglesworth Standard' (Whitaker House), P J Madden writes: "Smith stayed with the Army for several years. He saw that they had God's power, which he fervently desired. During their fiery prayer meetings, many people would fall down under the power of the Holy Spirit for long periods, sometimes 24 hours."

Instances in the Bible include the arrest of Jesus when the soldiers fell backwards, John falling at Jesus's feet as though dead in the Book of Revelation and St Paul being struck to the ground on the Damascus Road. The common factor was the powerful presence of Jesus. Now, through the Holy Spirit, a similar thing is happening.

I advise people neither to 'force' a manifestation nor resist it. Many literally feel weak at the knees and appear to lose their bodily strength. I suppose the majority of cases of falling could be avoided, but you get the distinct impression the Spirit is coming upon you, so why resist him? Of course, we know he can move whatever our position, but it seems for a large number of people that God is able to deal with them better in this vulnerable state.

The important thing is to be open to God and allow him

to do what he wants with you. We wouldn't think of telling a surgeon how to remove a cancer from our body, yet how often do we tell God how to work in our lives?

Concern for what others may think is a barrier caused by pride, which is one of the key areas of our lives that the Lord is dealing with. Without humility and submission to God, the new wave of Pentecostal power will pass us by. I used to think we Pentecostals had it all when it came to the Holy Spirit. But God had a surprise in store for me when, after the simplest of prayers by a bishop, I fell to the floor rolling about in laughter under an Anglican baptismal font! It was a burning bush experience for me.

Many have asked where self-control, as a fruit of the Spirit, comes into all this. The answer is in the context of the verse in question (Galatians 5.22), which is contrasting the fruit of the Spirit with the works of the flesh. The self-control we are urged to exercise is over our sinful nature, which tends towards immorality, anger, jealousy, selfish ambition, drunkenness and the like. We are not expected to control bodily manifestations which are a response to the Holy Spirit's activity in our lives.

I always emphasise that we are looking for fruit, not manifestations, and the fruit of the Spirit of love, joy and peace has been witnessed in great abundance among countless Christians who have done 'carpet time' in this wonderful move of God. I know someone who has been on the floor dozens of times, yet seen little outward manifestation otherwise. But the drama has taken place on the inside – in the heart – where he has experienced a sea change in his attitude to others, with a greater love and patience than he has ever known. We've also seen the fruit of conversions with 18 people saved in one week alone!

When I was at Holy Trinity, Brompton, in the summer

of 1994, I hadn't a clue why people were shaking, rattling and rolling and jumping up and down. But I sensed the presence of God. Nothing made sense, but I looked at my heart and it was light. Before that it was heavy with responsibility and duty and doing things the right way. Now I don't care. The only thing I'm really concerned about is that my heart keeps in tune with God.

It's the fruit that convinces me that this is God at work. He is doing a new thing. And just as the disciples did not recognise Jesus walking on the water, he is now coming like a ghost, and we haven't seen him like this before. But the fruit is the best we've ever seen and it is for that reason we embrace it so vigorously.

Pilgrim's progress

Pentecostals have generally been suspicious of pilgrimages, perhaps associating them with 'high church' ritual or even another religion altogether – forgetting that our own roots are firmly embedded in such practices. If it weren't for faithful pilgrims, the 20th century Pentecostal outpouring would not have spread as it did to the far corners of the earth.

When the 'fire fell' on Alexander Boddy's church in September 1907 I'm sure it wasn't a haphazard choice of the Holy Spirit. Boddy had been seeking a new anointing for some time and in 1904 had made a pilgrimage to Wales. On his return he inspired his congregation with news of the wonderful way God was moving, and Boddy's earnest desire was finally fulfilled when the Holy Spirit was poured out just as on the Day of Pentecost. And though 'holy laughter' was one of the strange manifestations at the time, it was the tongues phenomenon that caused the most controversy. But people came to Sunderland and Azusa

Street from all over the world – and travelling wasn't easy in those days – as a result of which Pentecostal and charismatic believers today number an astonishing 600 million. And now it seems that the well of Holy Spirit blessing previously dug here has been unblocked and thirsty pilgrims are once again drinking of the living waters Jesus promised.

But it isn't just a question of geography. God needs a channel for his river of anointing and looks for a man who will facilitate the outpouring without getting in the way.

So what, you may ask, is the scriptural basis for pilgrimages. Well, God has often made his special presence felt in specific places. Jerusalem and Bethlehem spring to mind, along with various mountains - most notably the Mount of Transfiguration. And then there was the Ark of the Covenant.

Think of the wise men who travelled about a thousand miles to worship Jesus and when they realised they had reached their goal 'they rejoiced with exceeding great joy.'(Matthew 2:10) They say that wise men still seek Jesus and will travel a long way to draw closer to him. Those who are being most affected by the present move are coming to the meetings with a sense of total inadequacy and barrenness – and they are falling in love with Jesus all over again.

When the Holy Spirit was first poured out on the Day of Pentecost, they were all together 'in one place'(Acts 2:1). The disciples were from Galilee, but Jesus told them not to leave Jerusalem until they were endued with power from on high. Why did they have to stay in Jerusalem? Perhaps because it was a crossroads of the world and God wanted the gospel spread to all nations. Toronto Airport could hardly be more of a crossroads of the modern world.

Holy Trinity, Brompton, is on the road to Heathrow Airport, and Sunderland is easily accessible by road, air and sea.

A soaked sacrifice!

One of the questions asked about the current move of God is why people seem to need constantly to go back for more prayer. What is the scriptural precedent for it? Can't your needs be dealt with in one go? And what is this strange prayer we keep hearing: "More, Lord"?

First of all, the more people come forward for prayer and the more time they spend in God's presence, the more change is evident in their lives.

Heart surgery, even with God, is not a quick fix. Although you become a new person when you are born again, sanctification is a process which only begins at conversion. But those who hunger and thirst for righteousness shall be filled. It won't happen as a result of a one-off gesture on Sunday when God is not given another thought for the rest of the week. But those who are consumed with a passionate desire for more of God in their lives shall be filled. Vessels are usually valued only by what they contain and God is looking for empty ones. My constant prayer is, 'Keep me hungry and increase my thirst'. Previous revivals have fizzled out because people stopped being hungry.

A classic picture of the pre-conditions for revival is given in the account of Elijah's contest with the false prophets on Mount Carmel (1 Kings 18). The prophets of Baal offered up a dry sacrifice and it would not burn, though I realise it was also because they were false prophets. Elijah offered up a sacrifice thoroughly soaked

THE SUNDERLAND REFRESHING

by twelve large jars of water. It was indicative of the water
of the Spirit and of faith in a supernatural God – like the
poured-out Spirit. Four jars were at first poured onto it,
but Elijah said 'Do it again' and 'Do it a third time'.

After it had been thoroughly soaked, Elijah prayed and
the fire fell. And a three-year drought was soon over as a
cloud the size of a man's hand rose from the sea. The sky
grew black, heavy rain followed and the power of the Lord
came upon Elijah.

As Elijah ushered in revival – the people turned to the
Lord because he demonstrated the power of God – so the
spirit-filled church is preparing the way of the Lord now.
Jesus referred to John the Baptist as an Elijah whose
significance many did not recognise. So now the Holy
Spirit is preparing the church for the coming of Jesus, but
many are not recognising the significance of what is
happening.

Yet many others come acknowledging they are dry and
barren, which is a step in the right direction as long as they
are thirsty for God. But they then need to be thoroughly
soaked and immersed (literally baptised) in the Spirit, so
that the living waters Jesus promised will flow freely
through them. Ask God to do it again and again until you
become a burnt-up sacrifice, healed of hurt and pain, with
hearts circumcised of selfish desires.

We need to be strong for what lies ahead, for trouble as
well as blessing will follow. The powerful ministry of
Jesus provoked even more opposition than the ministry of
John the Baptist. The coming revival will shake the
nations. Now is the time to take advantage of this move of
refreshing and make room for the Spirit to flow, just as
Elijah dug a trench round the altar.

I think the use of twelve stones representing all the tribes of Israel to build the altar was also highly significant, as was the fact that twelve jars of water were poured onto it. They represent the unity of God's people, and there is something so beautiful about the breaking down of denominational barriers that is now occurring. I know some say it is actually causing division, but the coming of God in power has always caused division. Many of the religious leaders of Jesus's day – referred to by both Jesus and John the Baptist as 'a brood of vipers' – couldn't find anything good to say about him, and even said he was of the devil. In the same way today some prominent evangelical leaders have gone so far as to say the current move is satanic.

Yet, despite opposition, there is a growing supernatural welding together of hearts that love Jesus. And it's happening around a restored 'altar' of true worship, which sets the scene for the Spirit to flow. It's so important that worship is led with the utmost sensitivity if our meetings are to flow with the Spirit. You'll find there's an anointing on certain songs, including old ones. It isn't a time for family favourites, but for stirring hearts to new depths of worship.

Those who continue to watch from the sidelines need to consider the question Elijah posed: 'How long will you waver between two opinions?' If this move is of God, I urge you to embrace it. 'The god who answers by fire – he is God.' Baal's men went about 'frantically prophesying', but the fire fell on the thoroughly soaked sacrifice!

The presence of God

According to a report in Joy magazine, outgoing AOG superintendent Warwick Shenton was 'pole-axed' at the Sonrise conference, so much so that he was unable to lead the worship.

This is a phenomenon that has occurred at many of our meetings, particularly involving key leaders.

I've already mentioned how David Cartledge was struck dumb when invited to testify at SCC. Joy editor Peter Wreford had a similar experience - though he was able to say a few words – on one or two occasions.

Basically, it has to do with the presence of God, which is so powerfully felt that the human body can't cope. We need to remember that 'we have this treasure in jars of clay'. And so we are often unable to stand in his presence.

But though Warwick was rendered incapable of leading worship at Sonrise, the tangible presence of God caused the people to bow down in adoration without him – just as the shepherds and the wise men did at Bethlehem.

Unfortunately, worship too often degenerates into little more than a sing-a-long because man is in control. As a result there is no flow of the Spirit and therefore no experience of the presence of God. When the ark – which represented the presence of God – was brought into the temple at the time of Solomon, it is recorded that the priests 'could not perform their service' because of the glory of the Lord (2 Chronicles 5:14). However, it only happened after the priests consecrated themselves 're-gardless of their divisions' and the trumpets and singers 'joined in unison as with one voice to give praise and thanks to God'.

There are few things so powerful as God's people coming together in unity and worshipping like this. It's interesting that there were 120 priests, just as there were 120 disciples 'in one accord' in the upper room on the Day of Pentecost. Both represent the unity of the body of Christ, which is becoming more and more evident as the Holy Spirit continues to move in our meetings. As in the true body of Christ, there are Anglicans, Baptists, a charismatic Catholic, Brethren, House Church people, Pentecostals and others all worshipping together in harmony.

Paul instructs Timothy: 'I want men everywhere to lift up holy hands in prayer, without anger or disputing'(1 Timothy 2:8). When we are brought to complete unity the world will know that God loves them (John 17:23). And that's what it's all about!

It is worth noting that Michal, daughter of King Saul, despised David in her heart as he abandoned himself before the Lord. She felt his display was unseemly for one of her husband's station, and having been raised in the royal household she felt she knew all about the right way to behave.

And today, as the Lord revives the passions of his people, some may feel that they, too, know the king's ways and despise what they see. Michal's barrenness is a warning that we shouldn't be too hasty in our judgements.

As a final note, I would like to say to all those who have not manifested in a visible way, be encouraged. Outward manifestation is not the acid test of what God is doing in the heart. Many have not laughed, fallen down, shaken or jerked, but God has profoundly changed their lives.

Appendix B

Tips for ministry teams

It has been our aim during the renewal services in Sunderland to minister out of servanthood and not superiority. Our ministry team is composed of people whose desire above all is to serve the body of Christ. Because this has been our heart, we have been willing to turn up night after night over an extended period of time to love, care and pray for people we may never see again, and without any recognition.

Above all we are called to deny ourselves, take up our cross daily and follow our master, Jesus (John 14:12).

It seems almost unbelievable that we have been called to share in the ministry of Jesus, but we should expect to be involved in power encounters even more remarkable than those recorded in the New Testament. The anointing we have in our ministry times comes from Christ and does not lead to pride in status, but confidence in what Jesus can do.

However, there needs to be a single-mindedness and a willingness to lay down anything in self-sacrifice, free from worry about the opinions of men, to see God's will worked out in our ministry. Our old lives are totally ineffective, we need to die to ourselves and let God raise up in us only what he wants. He calls us to serve him joyfully and wholeheart-edly. True servants of God realise the joy of serving God and other people, rather than themselves and their own selfish desires. We instruct our team to ask themselves over and over again 'Am I willing evening after evening to pay the price of being a servant on God's behalf? Am I willing to sacrifice all I have to God and am I willing to do whatever he asks me to do for him, whatever the cost?'

The other area which the Lord has emphasised again and again is that we must never be too proud to get stuck in and do the little jobs which need to be done. No task should ever be regarded as too menial for God's servants, so our folk are encouraged not just to serve on the ministry team, but in whatever situation help is needed.

Most importantly of all, God wants to receive all the glory from all that we do for him. The enemy always appeals to that desire we all have to be 'something'. The fact of the matter is God cannot use 'somethings'. We need to come to a place where we realise we have nothing left of ourselves, and no more 'rights' because we have given everything to him. 1 Peter 5:6 reminds us that a humble attitude is necessary for all those who wish to be raised up by God.

Foolish people will always try to make a name for themselves, but this should never be the attitude of God's servants.

The anointing of God is birthed in humility and shines through brokenness. The story of Gideon is a wonderful reminder of this. It was as the army broke the pitchers that the light was able to shine through and defeat a massive enemy. Through our broken vessels, God can again shine his light to expose the darkness.

Above all we must protect the anointing and keep the oil

flowing. Primarily we need to be people of the word; as it becomes part of us we will have a resource within us to minister to other people effectively.

Our ministry team is encouraged to read and apply the following helpful suggestions given to us by the Toronto Airport Vineyard covering five areas:

> Ministry team requirements
>
> Practical tips when praying
>
> Tips on praying for people
>
> Tips for receiving ministry
>
> Tips for catching people

MINISTRY TEAM REQUIREMENTS:

1. **Attitude**   Come with a servant's heart, prepared to minister.

2. **Preparation of heart**   If you are coming directly from work pray in the car. If not, spend time in prayer and the word.

3. **Personal Hygiene**

   a.   Bad breath

   b.   Use a deodorant and if you are at work all day, bring soap, a deodorant (there is a marvellous selection at the chemists these days!) and a change of clothes.

4. **Clothes**   Wear clean, comfortable clothes

   Women   Dress modestly

   a.   No low dresses or tops

   b.   No mini-skirts

   c.   Wear a long dress, culottes or trousers

   d.   Wear leggings underneath

5. **Prayer**   Come half-an-hour early for prayer.

PRACTICAL TIPS WHEN PRAYING:

1. Generally, men should pray with men and women with women.

2. RELAX! Remember it's God who is doing the work, not us. This takes the pressure off us!

3. If you touch people when you pray for them do it gently <u>on their foreheads or hands</u> so that their focus remains on God.

   Do not rub or do anything else to annoy them.

   You can always pray with your hand slightly away from them.

4. Don't push anyone over or press them to the ground.

5. If you wave your hands do it gently, and preferably not in front of their face. Violent waving in front of someone will distract them.

6. When you are moving around try to only step over people's bodies, not their heads. Most people 'resting in the Spirit' are still aware of things around them, and even if their eyes are closed they will be aware of someone stepping over their face.

TIPS ON PRAYING FOR PEOPLE:

1. When praying for individuals watch closely what the Spirit is doing (John 5:19). If no manifestation of the Holy Spirit comes within a few minutes, it is often wise to simply allow that person to keep worshipping and come back later. We have found it is even advisable to say something like this: "I want you to stay in worship for a little while and I will be back to you later." Meanwhile, others will pray for them, or you can come back when you are done with the next individual.

2. When people fall in the Spirit (called 'resting in the Spirit'), keep praying for them. It seems that everyone wants to get up way too quickly. God continues to do work even when we are down on the floor. Sometimes it will be noticeable and other times it might be quiet and inward. Allowing people to get up too quickly seems to work against what the Lord wants to do.

3. Generally, it is helpful to have people stand to receive ministry. This seems to allow the Holy Spirit more freedom to move.

4. Be careful not to push people over. This is offensive and will backfire by causing people to grow resistant to the real thing.

5. Don't force ministry. If the Spirit is not doing something, relax and remember that there will always be another opportunity.

6. If the person is finding it difficult to receive you might help them by the following:-

    a. Help them to deal with a tendency to rationalise, with their fears, or with a loss of control.

    b. Calm their fear of loss of control by helping them know what to expect. For example, let them know that they will have a clear mind, that they can usually stop the process at any point if they want to, and that the Spirit comes in waves.

7. Pray Biblical prayers such as some of the following:-

    a. Come Holy Spirit

    b. Let the kingdom of God come on earth as it is in heaven

    c. Outpouring of the Father's love for them and for others

    d. A deeper revelation of the Father's love in Christ

    e. Anointing for service

    f. Release of the gifts and callings

    g. For God's light to shine in them and through them

    h. Note: 'More Lord' is just a shortened form of blessing what the Father is doing (from John 5:19).

8. If you are getting 'words of knowledge' pray Biblical prayers related to those words. AND PRAY POSITIVELY. For example pray 'Let your peace come' if they are anxious.

9. Some people have 'fear of falling' issues. Help them to sit down or to fall carefully, especially if they have back problems, fear of falling or are pregnant.

10. It's okay to talk to the person during the engagement process. Be sensitive.

11 If your hand or body is shaking, pray with hands slightly away from the person so as not to distract them.

12. Don't project what God has been doing with you on to the person you are praying for.

    For example, if you have been laughing, don't pressure them to laugh. Find out what God is doing for them and bless it.

13. Do not attempt to get into any deliverance ministry in the main meeting. Pray God's peace over them if the person begins to manifest anything other than God's dealings. Don't be afraid to ask for help. Suggest that the person sees their own minister or (with their minister's permission) makes a private appointment.

14. Encourage the people you pray for to put testimonies in written form immediately.

TIPS FOR RECEIVING MINISTRY:

1. Come humble and hungry. Forget preconceived ideas and what has happened to others.

2. Allow the Lord to touch your heart and then analyse it.

3. Face your fears:-

   a. The fear of deception

   b. The fear of being hurt again or not receiving at all

   c. The fear of losing control. (This can often be seen when people step backward rather than fall).

4. Focus on the Lord, not on falling. Give the Holy Spirit permission to do with you what he wants to do – you don't have to fall. Ministry team members are encouraged to pray God's word over anyone who confesses the following:-

   a. They think they're worthless, ugly and stupid: Genesis 1:26; Psalm 139:14.

   b. They'll never get over this grief, they'll have to live with it or die with it:
   Isaiah 61:3; Joshua 1:9; Isaiah 53:4.

   c. No-one loves them, especially God:
   John 3:16; Ephesians 2:4.

d. They think they are weak, helpless, shy, timid, inadequate: 2 Corinthians 12:9; Philippians 4:13.

e. They think the sins of their past are too great, they continually feel condemned and guilty: Romans 8:1; 1 John 1:9; Psalm 103:12; Philippians 3:13-14.

f. They are afraid of everyone and everything: Psalm 56:3; Psalm 118;6; 2 Timothy 1:7.

g. They are disappointed and discouraged: 1 Corinthians 5:7; Hebrews 10:23; Luke 18:1; Psalm 27:14.

TIPS FOR CATCHING PEOPLE:

1. Do not touch the person being prayed for, but reassure them that there is someone behind them.

2. You don't have to take a hold of their shoulders as if you are going to help God.

3. As the person moves down, move back and then facilitate their move.

4. Men – be careful when touching women.

5. Get them to fall back, not forward.

6. Catchers – ONLY catch, do not pray. Do not wave your hands, only stand and be ready to catch.

7. Please do not push or pull anyone over. God does not need any help and it will ultimately backfire.

8. Do not hold anyone up by grabbing their shoulders or upper back.